Memories of Margaret

First published in Great Britain by Chords Crush Cancer, 2023

www.linktr.ee/chordscrushcancer

Paperback ISBN: 978-1-3999-7408-0

Acknowledgements

I have been thinking of writing a book about my Chords Crush Cancer fundraising journey for a couple of years, but life always seemed to get in the way. Family, kids, home, work, event organising and of course planning a wedding! However, it's not every day that you will raise over £20,000 for a charity you hold so close to your heart, so I knew soon after my wedding that it was time to get my story written. So, on the 23rd of April 2023, a full seventeen days after the wedding, the journey began.

I'd like to say a huge thank you to Carly, my wife, for her unwavering love and support with not only my charity events but also in writing this book. She has never once questioned my decision to do so despite being freshly married and planning my 8th fundraiser all at the same time! I get so excited and passionate about fundraising in memory of Mum that sometimes I need holding back with all my ideas. She has been my rock and has the patience of a saint! Thank you to the triplets, Toby, Violet and Tulip for welcoming me into their lives and for the love they show me, being a stepdad to these kids is an incredible feeling and I can't wait to support them on their own journey through adult life.

Thank you to all the artists that have supported Chords Crush Cancer over the years, Davy Lewis, Andy Mills, Graham Clews, Rhi Moore, Rob Cooper, Simon Davies, The Beautiful Ways, Hot Rubber, The Shire-ish Rovers, Magic Martin and Clive's Caricatures. To Robbie, Hugsy and the Irish Crew, Big Dave and Andrea with her incredible array of hats that always seem to go missing at the end of the evening, Franko and Ellis, I salute you all.

Thank you to Mandy and Luke for the t-shirts and Jenny for all the wonderful graphics, posters, and promo designs – I'm the kind of person who wants things done yesterday, so your patience with me and all of my requests has been greatly appreciated!

Thank you to our venues, The Red Barn, The Dolphin and The Inn on the Green, especially Rachael who trusts me so much to take over her pub for one night every year! And of course, to the entire bar staff who work tirelessly keeping our audiences' glasses full – cheers!

Thank you to each and every one of you who has come along to one of our events, to those who have bought raffle tickets and bid on the auctions. Of course this wouldn't be possible without all the local and national companies who have supported me with prizes. I still can't quite believe how many celebrities have slid into my DM's with kind words and offers of support, it is all rather surreal.

Thank you to the media who have helped to spread our message; BBC Radio Shropshire, The Shropshire Star, Shrewsbury Now, What's On Shrewsbury, Shropshire What's On, The Shrewsbury Biscuit Podcast and Shropshire Magazine.

Thank you to Joe Lloyd for taking such fabulous photos that adorn the cover of this book, the photo shoot was quite an extraordinary day! Walking around my hometown of Shrewsbury being snapped in various locations, not to mention poses, lead me to feel quite the celebrity for a couple of hours. It certainly felt that way at Shrewsbury Railway Station where people waiting for their train were wondering who I was and what on earth I was doing being snapped walking up and down the platform multiple times to get the perfect shot!

Mark Fielden

Thank you to my sisters Helen and Sally for a great childhood growing up, the youngest child is never the most spoilt hey! And to Thomas, Lauren and Kieran; it is a genuine privilege to be your uncle. To my in-laws, Bob and Doreen, thank you for welcoming me into your family and stepping into the role of chief raffle ticket folders in mum's absence – this gives me such warmth to know that you now do the job that mum made her own!

Thank you to the whole team at Lingen Davies Cancer Fund. I'm now a well-known figure in the fundraising office and always given a warm welcome. Thank you for embracing my ideas and for giving me the freedom to make them come to life. I'm honoured to have been recognised by the charity with two awards for my fundraising via Chords Crush Cancer, and my certificates hang proudly on the wall at home, alongside my framed copy of Shropshire Magazine front cover of course!

Lastly to Mum and Dad, thank you for my loving upbringing, teaching me right from wrong and moulding me into the man that I am today. Writing this book has been an emotional rollercoaster and I hope that I have done you both proud.

Much love,
Mark.

For Mum

9th November 1941 – 18th March 2017

Mark Fielden

Contents

Prologue
1. Why raise money for charity?.............11
2. Margaret.............17
3. Lazy Days.............52
4. Fighting Spirit.............59
5. The Void.............63
6. Sally.............76
7. Chords Crush Cancer.............82
8. Strike Whilst the Iron is Hot.............102
9. Carly.............108
10. Third Time Lucky.............129
11. A Beautiful Way.............139
12. Bigger and Better.............147
13. The Pandemic.............152
14. Failure Does Lead to Success.............184
15. Community Ambassador.............196
16. Onward.............242

Prologue

Kind, considerate and caring are the three words that sum up my mother Margaret. She was always putting so many others before herself. My fundraising journey in her memory has been an emotional rollercoaster, packed with tremendous highs and the lowest of the lows. I've been driven forward by following the morals she taught me; to help and support others who need it most.

I hope that my story gives those on their cancer journey some hope; comfort to those who have lost a loved one, and ultimately to inspire the next generation of fundraisers.

If I can do it, why can't you? I'm nothing special, just a regular guy from Shrewsbury who wanted to make a difference, and in supporting Lingen Davies Cancer Fund with my Chords Crush Cancer events, I genuinely believe I have.

To give to others who need it most is a wonderful feeling, made even more special by doing it in memory of the person you loved most. You have left the most amazing legacy Mum.

Forever in my heart

Mark x

'Be the change you wish to see in the world.'

Mahatma Gandhi

1

Why raise money for charity?

We rarely give to charity without a motivator of sorts. When we have experienced something close to our heart, the loss of a parent, child illness, friend, or colleague, it is not uncommon to want to raise money for the charity that supported them. It is that personal connection and relatability that motivates us to want to fundraise. People care deeply about their personal passions and look for charities that not only support their causes but that they can trust. It's not just about the charity itself but the underlying cause that really drives people.

Fundraising is an important activity that helps people in need and achieves important goals. Fundraisers are often conducted to benefit charities, schools, and other organizations that are working to make a difference in their communities; they have the potential to bring people together from all walks of life in support of a common cause. People fundraise for various reasons, including raising awareness about an issue, to generate financial resources to support projects and programs, and to build relationships with individuals and organizations.

The funds raised through fundraising activities can be used for medical treatments, scholarships, community development initiatives, disaster relief efforts, and much more. Fundraising is also a great way to get community members involved in meaningful work. By organizing activities such as bake sales, car washes, or raffles that bring people together to support a cause they believe in, fundraisers can offer the chance to make a lasting impact on causes that matter.

People in the UK are very generous and often donate billions of pounds to charities each year. This has created what is almost certainly the strongest and most effective charity sector of any country in the world.

Giving to charity is by and large seen as a good and selfless act; so I ask myself, why is it while some people happily donate to a charity, others can turn a blind eye? Research carried out by charities shows that the most important reason to fundraise is in the memory of someone. However, many people prefer to give direct. Those who do raise money sometimes don't always get thanked properly. Fundraisers are much more valuable than someone giving a one-off gift so it's important for charities to recognise this and make sure they look after them well.

The charity that I chose to support, Lingen Davies Cancer Fund, has always been extremely supportive and thankful for my efforts. I first became a friend of Lingen Davies after our third event in 2018. This was the first time Carly and I had our photo taken with the giant cheque! I was then approached by them to feature on their website in June 2018 for National Volunteers Week, where they first shared my fundraising story. They provided collection boxes for our 4th event and we went again to the fundraising office for a photo with the giant cheque when handing over the money raised from Chords Crush Cancer 4.

I think the relationship started to grow after our 4th event; we got to know more of the team, added each other on social media and then went from there. When Anna started to work for Lingen Davies in 2021 she was immediately interested in my event and we shared a few emails before I was invited into the office for a chat. I'd say we have a great relationship with the charity now, with all the Chords Crush Cancer events that have taken place and Carly's sponsored running meaning she is also involved with them in her own way too. She also volunteered at Abbeyfest their gin and beer festival and took place in the inaugural Titty Trail. We are big supporters of Lingen Davies and they really are an important charity to us both.

Lingen Davies has regular events for fundraisers and not only does that show they are thankful but supports relationships with other fundraisers which can be a blessing when feeling stuck for ideas or feeling a little isolated in the fundraising world.

Lingen Davies was established in 1979 to bring cancer services to Shrewsbury and reduce the need for people from throughout Shropshire, Telford & Wrekin, and Mid Wales to have to travel further afield into the West Midlands for treatment. A fund to develop a treatment centre at The Royal Shrewsbury Hospital was launched by the then Mayor of Shrewsbury, Bernard Lingen and local accountant Frank Davies.

Anna Williams, Communications and Marketing Lead at Lingen Davies said "Since that time the charity has funded in excess of £20,000,000 worth of technology and equipment to enhance the services and treatment offered at the hospital. One of the larger projects was the creation of the dedicated Lingen Davies Cancer Centre which houses radiotherapy and chemotherapy services."

"Additional support services offered by the charity include funding for the iCan Cancer Rehabilitation course, complimentary therapies offered by Severn Hospice, and a wide-range of other items including radar keys for patients to access public facilities, mirrors in clinic rooms for patients, technology and software to enable more efficient treatment planning, additional capacity items for pathology and dermatology, smart TVs for those patients in isolation wards – sometimes for up to three months at a time, and a new cooling cap for chemotherapy."

"We also fund the 'Live Life Cancer Awareness Project' which sees colleagues interacting with the wider public at summer shows, town markets, private organisations and local social events. By sharing information about the signs and symptoms of cancer we intend to encourage more people to seek guidance from their GP and bring about more early diagnoses."

"Charities rely on people like Mark to ensure they are able to keep doing the work they do – often lifesaving work for vulnerable members of society. Without fundraising the charity would not be able to enhance the care and treatment of the 4000+ new patients who come through the doors of the Cancer Centre every year; in addition to those with ongoing treatment such as immunotherapy."

"Without fundraising, the charity would be unable to raise awareness about cancer in the wider community, and it would not be able to support those living with and beyond cancer to readjust to a 'normal' life. Fundraising means we are in a position to do things for local cancer patients that the NHS simply does not have the budget for."

"Mark became a Friend of the charity when he organised the very first Chords Crush Cancer event in 2016" added Williams. "Since that time Mark has been a regular visitor to the fundraising office, and is a brilliant ambassador and fundraiser for Lingen Davies. Personally, I met Mark when I started at the charity in 2021, he was one of the first fundraisers I had the pleasure of working with and supporting with Chords Crush Cancer."

2

Margaret

Margaret Fielden, Mum, was born in Shrewsbury on 9th November 1941. She grew up living at Brighton Terrace in Bradford Street with her mother Kathleen and was the youngest sibling to Bridget, Peter and Pat. Attending the Cathedral School on Town Walls she was often home first whilst the rest of the family were out working so it was her job to light the fire! She took this role so seriously that it actually led to a court appearance! When she received a coal delivery, she would count the coal bags into the shoot. One day she noticed that the coalman could not count as well as her, she reported this to her mother who challenged it and they celebrated victory in the courts.

Mum met Tony, my Dad, at a dance at The Lion Hotel. The Lion Hotel is a Grade I listed, 16th century, former coaching inn, and is located in the heart of Shrewsbury. In the 1950s through 60s, every weekend there was 'Saturday night dancing'. Dad saw Mum there and finally plucked up the courage to ask her for a dance, to which she agreed.

After their dance, Dad asked her if she wanted a drink, however, he had taken so much time in waiting to ask her to dance that by the time they got to the bar, it was closed!

Margaret and Tony married on 18th April 1970 at Our Lady of Pity Church, in Shrewsbury with a wedding reception held afterwards at The Shropshire Lad.

Shrewsbury is a beautiful place and it is no wonder why Mum spent her whole life there. It sits 9 miles east of the Welsh border and is a market town in the county town of Shropshire, and sits on the River Severn. The town has Saxon roots and the centre has a largely undisturbed medieval street plan with over 660 listed buildings including some from the 15th and 16th centuries. Shrewsbury Castle, a red sandstone fortification was founded in 1074 by the Earl of Shrewsbury, Roger de Montgomery. It is the birthplace of Charles Darwin and had a role in nurturing aspects of English culture such as drama, ballet, and pantomime.

Working life saw Mum as a clerical assistant for Post Office Engineering based in Mardol which later moved to Telephone House. She would pass her time reading her book, until the supervisor came to check up on her. She tried to avoid the supervisor by having extended breaks in the toilets to chat with her colleagues until she was caught and received a telling off!

When my parents started a family, Mum stayed home to raise me and my sisters, Helen and Sally, but she also worked as a childminder where she looked after many children. In addition to being a childminder and as we grew, she went on to become a playschool assistant, a swimming club teacher and even helped out with school dinners.

The kids used to love her helping with the school dinners as she wouldn't force them to eat everything on their plate – unlike the other dour dinner ladies!

Mum was always one for her soaps, I remember her watching Coronation Street religiously and we kids always knew it was bedtime for us when it had finished! She also liked watching the football, darts and other sports. She enjoyed listening to Jim Reeves; he was one of her favourite singers.

I attended secondary school at The Priory School, just across the road from our family home, which is a good school that I really enjoyed attending. Mum and Dad would always come along to parents evening and were very supportive, they had no need to worry though as I was a good student, never got a detention! I never dared to!!

In reality though our upbringing was so good that we were not naughty kids, we followed our parent's beliefs and they were always there to guide and support us. Mum actually played netball for a team years before I was born at the same school, on the courts that would become our Tennis and Netball courts. I've watched this footage on 'Cinefilm.' Dad had a Cinefilm camera that he used to record events on; these are absolutely amazing to watch back.

Mum was also a huge animal lover. As a kid she had a pet tortoise called Michael! She used to polish his shell with lavender polish, let him outside for exercise in the garden and generally spoil him rotten. I remember growing up that we had a bunny rabbit, cats, dogs, goldfish, budgies and even a cockatiel. I asked for a parakeet one birthday so I could teach it to talk, however I ended up with a cockatiel called Tufty who would only whistle!

There was a footballer at the time playing for Shrewsbury Town called Dean Spink, who had his own chant 'Deano, Deano, Deano, do-do, do-do, do-do' which Mum thought was hilarious when she taught Tufty to whistle it as well as the classic Wit-woo! He would whistle for hours, so much so that we had to place a tea towel over the cage to shut him up when we were trying to watch the TV.

She has been known to be called "Mrs Want" by my Dad and I was "Mr Want!" Once Mum put a picture of a puppy on the bathroom mirror so that Dad would see it every time he was shaving! Yes, you guessed it Mum won! The dog is called Benji and still lives with Dad today.

Mum liked to keep busy, helping out at the Shrewsbury & District Stroke Club as we grew up. She found out about it through the Church and was asked if she and Dad would help to support it. They would attend monthly meetings to play Bingo, listen to guest speakers and join in with musicians who had been booked to perform. They also went on day trips to various places such as Llandudno, enjoying a walk around and a nice meal. Mum always liked helping people and often got involved with local activities. She would make pies, jam and of course her world-famous chocolate cake.

I've often wondered where I get my fundraising genes from. I've certainly followed the morals that Mum taught me when I was growing up and I may well have inherited her love for helping others that are in need too. Mum would be the first to help at any event that was raising money for a cause.

My earliest memories are from jumble sales, that I was taken along to either be a help or hindrance at! These would raise money for the Church, it's so strange to think now how rare a jumble sale has become, I'm sure that some of today's generation will not have even heard of one!

Yearly sales in Shrewsbury Town Square would also take place to raise funds for the Church, various stalls including bric-a-brac, tombola, books and cakes were all present but I remember Mum being on the stall where you could win a football or a teddy bear. It was like tombola but you had to pick ticket out of a bucket and when opened it would tell you if you were a winner. I had great fun on that stall with Mum and my sisters.

Another memory is McDonalds, now most people are familiar with a Big Mac or Chicken McNuggets but not many will remember the orange drink, it tasted so good! McDonalds would donate a drinks machine to fundraising events and large cartons of their orange syrup drink. At the event the syrup would then be mixed with water and dispensed from the machine into McDonald's cups that they also provided, for a bargain 5p. The drink tasted so good and we used to sell cup after cup! Kids of today just don't know what they missed out on!

Mum was very religious and growing up Our Lady of Pity church in Harlescott, Shrewsbury played a big part in family life. It is where mum and dad got married, where we were christened, the place my sister Sally got married to Nev, and ultimately where mums final swansong was held, her funeral in the building she had served so well over many years.

Mum was always busy with the church, she would sell greeting cards from a stall at the back of the church, help maintain and clean the church for large ceremonies, and along with her sister Pat organise the flowers for Easter and Christmas. She was the 'go to' person at the Church, the 'familiar face' that everyone knew and loved.

She was very friendly with Priest Desmond Friel and his housekeeper Pauline, and would often go to their house after church for coffee. Mum would always go to midnight mass on Christmas Eve and loved singing the hymns and carols. She loved singing so much that she would often get everyone else singing too.

My memories of church life start with preparing for my first holy communion, attending the weekly church service and then going to study at my mentor's house. There were a few of us learning about the church and religion led by three sisters, who like mum, were devout church goers and dedicated to Our Lady of Pity church. After weeks of training, we were ready to attend church and receive our first holy communion, the body and blood of Christ. I attended the church service, dressed smartly in white shirt, red tie and matching red sash, proudly wearing my holy cross around my neck.

My Holy Communion

Mark Fielden   25

I remember feeling a mixture of nerves and excitement to be fully entering into church life, receiving Holy Communion, in front of my proud family and friends that I had completed the pre-communion preparation with. After the service we attended a local school hall for a celebration, with lots of photographs taken and plenty of food from the scrumptious buffet.

I attended church with my family every Sunday morning, after my first holy communion, and quickly settled into church life, joining in with prayers and belting out the hymns at the top of my voice! My uncle Peter served on the altar, and I soon took a keen interest in what he did and wondered if it was something that I could do with him.

The priest agreed to my request, and it was not long before I was attending altar boy training so that I could join my uncle every Sunday. As an Alter boy you are responsible for assisting the priest to make sure that the service runs smoothly. You lead the priest onto the Altar, carry the candles, hold the bible for the readings, help with the preparation of the bread and wine and ring the bell!

An Altar server often rings a small bell during the consecration, to draw attention to the precise moment when transubstantiation – the conversion of the bread and wine into the body and blood of Christ – takes place.

I completed my training and was ready to take my place on the altar alongside my uncle and the other Alter servers. I remember putting my cassock, which are vestments that Alter servers wear, on for the first time ready to take part in my first church service. As I was the newest member within the church sacristy, I was not yet experienced enough to ring the bell, but I was trusted to carry a candle onto the Altar and really enjoyed my first experience of being an Altar boy.

Over the months and years that followed I became a more senior member within the sacristy and experienced all, bar one, element of the church service throughout the various celebrations within the church calendar. I say bar one, as I was never allowed to use the thurible, the metal censer in which incense is burned during the service, as that was my Uncle Peter's job! I was allowed to prepare the incense for the thurible, but never actually got my hands on it to use it!

Mark Fielden   27

There were many prestigious services that I took part in during my time as an altar boy. Hosting the cannon at our church, the annual outdoor services at the remains of Haughmond Abbey, Easter, but it was Midnight mass on Christmas Eve that was always my favourite. The atmosphere inside the church on this night was always electric, full of warmth, love and excitement.

Our family built up a close relationship with the priest and his housekeeper, Father Desmond Friel and Pauline Clarkson, during the time that they were at Our Lady of Pity. We would spend time with them away from the church which created a special bond and happy memories. From them both visiting us on holiday at Pontins in Southport, to Sunday lunch at each other's houses, meals out at the pub to even buying a couple of dogs together! Mum wanted a dog and so did Pauline, and after much pestering from them both, they succeeded in their wish. We had Shandy, a Sheltie, and Pauline and Desmond had his brother who they named Sandy! The brothers were wonderful dogs and loved it when we would all meet up to take them on walks together.

My favourite memory is when we used to go and play snooker at a local hotel. They had a full-sized table which they allowed us to use, and I really started to develop my game, maybe we were going there too often! Desmond always used to pay for the light meter, it was 50p for 30 minutes, and he always used to let me keep any remaining coins that were left over when it was time for us to go home. Looking back, learning how to play snooker so young lead me into really enjoying playing pool in my teens and younger adult life.

After many years as priest of Our Lady of Pity, Desmond and Pauline were posted to a new church in Hattersley, on the outskirts of Manchester. The whole church community was devastated that we were losing a wonderful priest and a fantastic woman in Pauline. It hit our family harder than most, as they were now classed as close family friends, but we vowed to keep in touch, and it was not long before we went up to visit them. Car packed, kids in the back, dog in the boot and mum in the front, dad drove us to their new church for a weekend stay.

It was fantastic to see them, the dogs certainly loved seeing each other again, and it was great to look around their new home. I remember it being on the large side, with plenty of space for us to all stay over, but imagine my surprise when I walked into one room downstairs to find a snooker table! I spent hours practicing against Desmond, dad and my sister Helen, and the best bit was I didn't need 50p for the light as there was no meter!

As the years passed and I got older, I moved away from church life as Sunday morning football started to take over! I would still attend church with mum and the family on a Saturday evening, but on a less regular basis, and I stepped away from the altar serving as it really wasn't for me anymore. Mum remained a regular at services and kept in touch with Desmond and Pauline, visiting them in Oswestry on numerous occasions, which was their next church posting after Hattersley.

Sadly, Desmond and Pauline have both passed away, but I remember the great memories of the times we shared, the many laughs that we had along the way, their love and kindness towards our family, and the two wonderful dogs whose brotherly love was infectious.

Although I no longer consider myself to be religious, I do believe that there is something in terms of an afterlife and Our Lady of Pity church will always hold special memories for me. To be back up on the altar in front of the lectern, where years earlier I had served as an Altar boy, at mum's funeral delivering the eulogy, was a surreal experience, but one that I will remember for the rest of my life.

Mum was a huge Shrewsbury Town Football Club fan and would go to matches at the Gay Meadow Stadium with her sister Pat and brother Peter to watch the games, and in particular her favourite player Arthur Rowley. It was her love and passion for the team that drew me to support the club from an early age.

I remember going along with Mum and Dad to a few games watching on from the Family Stand and instantly I was hooked! We moved from the Family Stand when I became a teenager and moved into the Centre Stand where we all held a season ticket for many years. Our seats were by the players' tunnel and just above the home dugout, so a great view and also close to the players as they came on and off the pitch. I remember leaning over the side of the tunnel to try and get a 'high-five'.

Mark Fielden   31

My earliest memory of watching football on the TV was the World Cup which was held in Mexico 1986, so I would have been 7 years old. From that moment on I was hooked and my love affair with the game and Shrewsbury Town really took off.

There is nothing quite like the feeling of going to watch a live match, the excitement of putting your replica shirt on and heading to the ground, buying the match day programme and then once inside the stadium, straight to the buffet! I was never one to have Bovril, though I did enjoy a pasty and a hot chocolate on match days. Times and pre-match routines changed as I became older, ditching the hot drink in favour of a pint in the pub before the game, no matter how old you are though the same feeling and buzz inside your stomach still exists, hoping that your team will get the right result and score a hat full of goals along the way!

Approaching the old Gay Meadow with Mum and Dad I often saw people selling a magazine that was not the official programme; one day my inquisitive nature got the better of me and I purchased a copy of 'A Large Scotch' (ALS), the Shrewsbury Town supporters' magazine, dubbed a fanzine by supporters.

A fanzine is an unofficial publication, not affiliated to a club, and written by supporters of their team. It's usually 'tongue in cheek' and very close to the bone, giving fans the opportunity to air their anger and frustration when things are not going well on the pitch, but equally to shout from the rooftops how good your team is when you are at the top end of the league table! I really enjoyed reading ALS and bought a copy every time I saw it on sale, very good value at just 50p. My frustration was that I wanted to read it on a regular basis, but due to being compiled by supporters who had full time jobs the issues produced was very sporadic.

I decided that I was going to start writing my own fanzine, dedicated to Shrewsbury Town, and spent some time researching similar publications from different clubs in the football pyramid. One that sticks to mind was a Nottingham Forest fanzine called 'Forest Forever.' This was written by a 15-year-old lad and was absolutely brilliant. It had the right mix of articles coupled with some fantastic cartoons to illustrate each story.

I was inspired to start writing the fanzine after regularly reading 'When Saturday Comes' (WSC) magazine. This is a monthly magazine that was first published in London in 1986. It aims to provide a voice for intelligent football supporters, offering both a serious and humorous view of the sport, covering all topics that fans are likely to talk about, whether serious or trivial. It had a fanzine directory in the back of each issue where they would complete reviews; my aim was to make it into WSC!

I asked Mum if I could borrow her typewriter and got to work, writing different articles about the club, players, latest results, basically anything that I thought fellow supporters would find interesting. It was hard going typing on the typewriter, but as I didn't own a computer I made do and soon enough I had finished my first edition of 'The Mighty Shrew.'

Mum and dad arranged for it to be photocopied and then helped me put the pages in order and staples in the spine, I remember dad buying me a long arm stapler to make this task a little easier! I'm not exactly sure how many copies we had, maybe around 50, but I was super excited for the next home game and to start selling my fanzine.

On arrival at the ground, we set up our position by the main entrance so that the supporters would have to walk past us as they made their way to the stadium. We made a slow start, a solitary few fans parting with their 50p's to purchase a copy, when we were suddenly approached by bloke saying, "You can't sell that here."

From memory, I believe he was the editor of the official match day programme and didn't want his sales affected by fans buying my magazine! We moved away from directly outside the stadium and set up our second pitch of the day on the corner of the street that led from the main road towards the ground. This worked an absolute treat for us and issue one of 'The Mighty Shrew' was a sell out!

My emotions were all over the place that day, from nervousness that nobody would buy a copy, to anger at being told I could not sell it, to elation that we had sold out and then finally excitement upon entering the stadium to watch my team play.

Mum and dad bought me a PC so that I could continue with my writing journey and editions two and three soon followed. It was so much easier using a word processor to compose my articles rather than selecting the right keys on the old typewriter. Editing mistakes was also so much easier, rather than getting the Tipp-Ex out and waiting for it to dry before starting to type again! My writing style became more in depth and as my confidence started to grow. I made the switch to getting the fanzine printed professionally. Spending hours on end, day after day writing articles, proof reading and setting up the layout, was made worthwhile when the box full of fanzines arrived back from the printers!

The fanzine was growing in popularity, and we had extended our print run to 200 to keep up with the demand. I started offering a subscription service for exiled fans where they could pay for three editions in advance, and I would post them out to them. I got a big break when Sports Pages decided to sell it!

Sports Pages was a book shop, with branches in London and Manchester, whose remit was to sell sports books, newspapers and fanzines on as broad a range of sports as possible. John Gaustad, the Sports Pages' shop founder, is said to have launched it in 1985 after he was unable to find any sports books about his beloved All Blacks in London.

I visited Sports Pages in Manchester, later in life when I was visiting a friend at University, and it was quite surreal to see my Shrewsbury Town fanzine in there, amongst the likes of Manchester United, Liverpool and Arsenal supporters' magazines! 'The Mighty Shrew' is also featured in the National Football Museum, under the Shrewsbury Town section. Imagine my surprise when I received a text message from a friend who was visiting it with an image of my magazine! Simply unreal!

I had started to include player interviews and would often write to them at the club hoping to get a reply. The range of answers to my questions was quite staggering to say the least. Paul Edwards, the Shrewsbury Town goalkeeper, sent me a lovely hand written reply answering every question that I asked, at the time he was the PFA Representative for the club, so you could really pick up on his professionalism, whereas one of his team mates just took me for a pint!

I had invited local lad, Kevin Seabury, to answer some of my questions for an upcoming edition and he agreed to meet for a chat. We ended up going to a pub in the town centre, got the questions done and dusted in less than half an hour, then proceeded to chat football and drink beer! What a fantastic afternoon that was!

In all I produced sixteen editions of the fanzine over a number of years, going out on a high with a full colour cover that looked really professional, some fans even mistook it for the match day programme!

Whilst Mum went to every home game, it was rare that she would join me and dad on the coach to the away ones. However, when the Shrews made it to Wembley in 1996, she made an exception and joined us on the long journey to the capital.

As regular members of the 'Away Travel Club,' following the team all over the country, dad was asked to be a steward in charge of one of the coaches for the trip to the National Stadium. This involved collecting the fare, conducting the raffle, selling the Wembley edition of the fanzine, and of course collecting a tip for the driver on the way home. Dad did a brilliant job, he seemed to enjoy it and his only real struggle was choosing which video to put in the VHS player to entertain the supporters during the long drive!

It was my first experience of Wembley, which was huge compared to all the other grounds that I had visited, but sadly the team did not perform on the day, and we ended up on the wrong end of a 2-1 score line. Ironically a certain Nigel Jemson scored both goals for Rotherham on the day; he'd sign for Shrewsbury many years later and dump Everton out of the FA Cup with a wonder free kick, which gave him forgiveness from the Town fans!

Mark Fielden   39

There have been many memories made over the years travelling the length and breadth of the country supporting the Town. Thousands of miles covered, and many coaches sat on dreaming of victory to seal a perfect away day. One vivid memory of supporting the Town on the road was when I was still at school. I left early for a 'dentist' appointment so that I could make the bus on time for the trip to Blackburn Rovers. It was the Coca Cola Cup 3rd round and Shrewsbury were up against a Rovers team managed by Kenny Dalglish, flying high in the Premier League with a wealth of talent to choose from. Alan Shearer, Mike Newell, Stuart Ripley, Graeme Le Saux, Colin Hendry and Tim Sherwood all spring to mind. Shrewsbury, playing in their away strip of red, were fantastic on the evening showing plenty of passion to earn a reply after a hard earned 0-0 draw. Upon leaving Eewood Park that evening our coach broke down on the Motorway on the way back to Shropshire. We were all stuck at a service station for hours as we waited for a replacement coach to arrive to take us home. I only managed a couple of hours sleep in bed that night, after we finally made it home, before it was time to get up and head for school, tiredness being my punishment for leaving the previous day early for the 'dentist' trip I guess!

Shrewsbury Town had reached the League Two Play-Off Final in the 2008/2009 season, taking on Gillingham at Wembley stadium, but mum, dad and I were going on holiday. No sooner had we got seated in the minibus that collected us from home, mum had already asked for the radio to put on BBC Radio Five Live so that we could listen to the match! Listening to a match is very different from watching on TV or being in the stadium, so it was quite a tense ride to the airport that day. Sadly, the Town lost 1-0, promotion denied for another season at least, but we managed to listen to the game and not let it dampen our holiday spirits too much as we boarded the plane for some much needed time in the sun!

The club finished the 2010–11 seasons in 4th place, missing automatic promotion by only 1 point. The following 2011–12 season they finished 2nd on 88 points. They won 1–0 over Dagenham & Redbridge to achieve promotion to League One after a 15-year absence. Shrewsbury exceeded expectations the following 2012–13 season and ultimately managed to seal League One safety with two games to spare of their first season back finishing 16th. Shrewsbury were promoted back to League One on 25th April 2015.

Following disruption to the season in March 2020 due to COVID-19, final League One standings were decided on a point's per game basis with Shrewsbury finishing in 15th place. In November 2020, Ricketts was sacked with Shrewsbury in 23rd place and was replaced by Steve Cotterill who was replaced by the current manager Matt Taylor in 2023.

During my younger years' football was a big part of my life, I played junior league level for Monkmoor Comits and then progressed to play for Shrewsbury Area Schools and Shropshire County. Mum and Dad would come to watch me at every game, Dad recording on his video camera and Mum providing the half time coffee for the other spectators. She had this massive flask; it was like a barrel with a tap that would serve endless coffee for the other watching parents! She was such a big supporter of mine when it came to football. I played in goal and always wanted the latest keeper's gloves; they were always the most expensive! Mum would often badger Dad into letting me have them!

I've always been interested in football for as long as I can remember. I started to go to football training every Saturday morning between 10am and 12pm at Belvidere School; ironically this is where the kids now go to school. It was run by a club called Monkmoor Comits.

I would have been around 9 years old when I started playing for the team at Under 10's level and I stayed with them all the way through until Under 16's. The club was run by a guy called Jim Mitchell and the coach was Ray Coles, again it's quite ironic that Mr Coles is now the kids PE teacher at the same school! I used to love to get muddy so goalkeeper was a natural position for me. They say you have to be a bit crazy to go in goal but I absolutely loved it! We were never the best team, but we turned up every week for training on the Saturday and then play matches in the Shrewsbury Junior League every Sunday. It was great fun with no pressure and thoroughly enjoyable.

Mark Fielden   43

Our manager Brian Binnersley was a fantastic bloke, and he built a really strong team spirit within the team. At the end of every season there would be the presentation evening at a local hotel, where all the teams from the different age groups would be presented with a trophy for playing, and then there were the main awards ups for grabs - most improved player of the year, players player of the year and the coveted managers player of the year.

The family and I would attend every year and I was always excited to see if I would win an award. Dad always used to joke that you got a trophy 'for turning up' which looking back now I guess he was right, but it was still a great feeling to be recognised for playing. I won more than my fair share of the main awards during my time with the club, but if I'm honest I was disappointed the times when I did not come away with one of the main awards!

I was certainly confident in my ability as a goalkeeper and was one of the best players in the team, often being called 'The Cat' by our opponents due to my shot stopping abilities! Mum and Dad used to wind me up saying that I only won the main awards so that I would not leave to join another club.

On more than one occasion, I had the opportunity to join one of the better teams in the league, but I enjoyed playing with my mates with less pressure; we were just a group of lads who got on well with each other and were allowed to enjoy our football. I still managed to play for the team and got my opportunities to play for Shrewsbury Area Schools, Shropshire FA and was snapped up by Shrewsbury Town Football Club School of Excellence, so I didn't do too badly over the years!

I remember when Mum and Dad received a hand-written letter asking for my services. There had been a new team join the league, having been formed the previous season, and their Manager Dave Leddington wrote to Mum and Dad asking for me to sign for them. We discussed it but I didn't really want to leave Monkmoor Comits where I was happy and enjoying my football. It's funny to look back on now with how the football world is, you can never imagine a manager writing a letter to a player's parents asking to sign their son. I'm sure Mum and Dad might have had different thoughts on my decision had a transfer fee been involved!

Playing for Monkmoor Comits was really great fun, the training sessions at Shrewsbury Town School of Excellence were far more serious, although the facilities we had back then were nowhere near what the young players get today.

Mark Fielden   45

We would train at the football ground once a week, the sessions were held by the STFC youth coaching staff and it was always great when some of the first team players came to a session to take part.

We would get changed in the 1st team dressing room but that's about as glamorous as it got. There was a gravel car park at the back of the Gay Meadow ground where we would train during the winter months, this was lit by a couple of lights which wasn't ideal and when wet you would get absolutely filthy! Goalkeeper training was miles away from where it is today, the warm up would comprise of you kicking the ball against the wall of the away end and then try and catch it, it's crazy when I think about it now but that's how it was!

I was with Shrewsbury Town right up until the age of 16, I really dreamed that one day I would become a professional footballer but sadly it was not meant to be.

Over the years the club and training became more professional; we moved away from the car park to a fully floodlit Astroturf pitch which was much better, we had proper goalkeeping training from the youth team players and coaches which was brilliant and we started to be assessed.

I remember forging a close relationship with the youth team keeper at the time, Tony Grenham, and really enjoyed the training sessions that he put on for us. I played a few matches for the School of Excellence against local teams but there was never a league structure like there is today. It was all rather sporadic and we could go months without a game, so I was happy to still be playing for Monkmoor Comits every Sunday to get my competitive football fix!

My big break came when I was selected to play for the Youth Team when I was at the School of Excellence. I remember being called to one side after training and being asked if I was available to play. Wow, of course I was available; if I made a good impression here then this could be my stepping stone to being offered a Youth Training Scheme contract at the club and a step closer to playing for my hometown team.

I was named as substitute for the game and handed the number 13 shirt, which I excitedly changed into in the dressing room before the game. I remember being struck by how much more professional the Youth Team set up was before a game. The kit was all laid out in the changing room, including a black slip! What was this for I wondered? I soon found out that it's what you wear under your shorts, whereas I was used to just playing in my boxer shorts under my goalkeeper shorts! We were given a rub down by the physio whilst the manager went through the tactics for the game and the threat from the opposition. It was at this point I was told that I would come on at half time and take over in goal from Tony, the guy who had trained me for the last couple of years; I was excited but very nervous.

The team were not playing well and were 2-1 down at half time when I came into the line-up. I was always very vocal as a goalkeeper shouting to my defence and organising them into the correct position. It felt strange shouting at teammates who were older than me and who I had never played with before, but I was there to do a job. I also noticed how much quicker the pace of the game was compared to what I was used to in the Sunday League and the velocity of the shots coming my way was also far superior!

The manager had told the team at half time that if we lost this game then they would all be in for extra training in the morning, which was due to be their day off. That ramped up the pressure on me and the rest of the team. We got an equaliser late on in the half and then came my big moment, their striker was through on goal, bearing down towards me, one versus one, he sprinted into the 18-yard box and smashed the ball high towards my left, I honestly thought it was passed me but I leapt to my left and turned the ball around the post, what a save and what a moment! The game ended in a 2-2 draw which meant a clean sheet for me and no extra training for the lads. In the dressing room after the game they all came rushing up to me exclaiming what a save, it was a brilliant feeling. Tony gave me some good words of advice and said how well I had played.

Sadly, that was the only time I got to play for the Youth Team, a few weeks later I was handed my assessment letter after training saying that the club would not be taking up the option of a YTS with me. I was absolutely gutted. My work in training and performance in that game were recognised but sadly it was not enough, I was not considered good enough or tall enough to be a goalkeeper, or to be given the opportunity to take on the YTS and follow my dream of becoming a professional footballer.

After being released by the Centre of Excellence I continued to play for Monkmoor Comits and undertook a referee's course to officiate junior league matches. I was a ref for a full season, but it was something that I never really enjoyed to be honest; I much preferred the excitement of playing and pulling off saves to keep the opposition out! I remember the first decision I made in my first match as a ref, I gave the throw in to the wrong team, it was a clear and obvious error but I stuck by my decision. Refereeing was just not for me!

Whilst playing for Shropshire we played against a team from Deeside who had a certain Michael Owen in their team; yes the former Liverpool, Real Madrid, Newcastle, Manchester United and England star. I saved a penalty against him that day which I will never forget. Mum was standing on the side line watching, super proud as always. We lost that game 11-1 I think but hey, I still saved his penalty!

I often use this memory as my 'claim to fame' moment at work training days when you have to stand up and introduce yourself, all the time wondering if he remembers me?!

After junior football I progressed to playing for a pub team at the age of 17. I was not old enough to play without consent from parents as I was not 18, Mum fully supported me, writing a letter to the Sunday League with her approval, and would be watching along with my Dad and sisters on the side-line. She even washed the team kit every week! Something that Dad often moaned about saying "It would wear the washing machine out with all the mud!"
Mum always cleaned my boots for me and would wash my keeper's gloves in the bathroom sink, she was not afraid of the mud!

During my younger years, Under 10's to Under 14's, we used to have a match at the end of the season with the kids taking on the parents. Mum was one of the first names on the team sheet and was not afraid to put a hard tackle in! Luckily I was in goal so I missed out on her strong tackling skills!

Mark Fielden

3

Lazy Days

As a family we always used to go to Pontins for our summer holiday. We went to various resorts in the UK - Southport and Minehead spring to mind. I have wonderful memories of these. We used to arrive early so that we could have lunch in the cafe, always sausage, chips and beans for me! Then queue up in the ballroom to collect the key to the chalet. We used to do it all, swimming in the day, rides around the park on the '4 person bikes'; day trips out to the beach, playing on the rides at the park - such fun times. But it was in the evenings when we would have the most fun.

Every evening we would head to the ballroom for bingo and the kid's entertainment "Kids Club" where games would be played until it was time for bed for the younger kids, when we sang the song "Good Night Children, See You in the Morning." Mum and Dad used to allow us to stay later and we would enjoy a Slush Puppie whilst watching the other entertainment, mostly live music from the house band or a cabaret show from the Bluecoats who were fantastic.

Family swimming at Pontins pool

One of my Birthdays

Mark Fielden

One memory I will never forget is when they had live wrestling in the evening. We were sat close to the ring and I shouted "booooooo" to one of the wrestlers who nearly jumped out of the ring to come and get me. I hid under the table and grabbed onto Mums leg for her to protect me!

As we got older we went on our first holiday abroad. We went to Lanzarote with Mums sister Pat and husband Bryan, their son Dave and Mum, Dad, Helen, Sally and me. I was so excited. I remember Mum and Aunty Pat leading the camels down the volcano as the rest of us were riding them. I recall the dreaded 'Time Shares' where people would ship you off in a bus to a resort and try and get you to buy a time share. Mum, Dad, Aunty Pat and Uncle Bryan used to love this as they would get a free meal and often a free gift; they even received a Walkman one time! However, they never had any intention of purchasing a time share!

After our trip to Lanzarote we went on holiday abroad on a yearly basis. Lanzarote was a firm favourite where we would hire a Villa, but we also visited Gran Canaria, Tenerife and Menorca. Mum would usually find a stray cat to befriend and add some cat food into the shopping basket at the local 'Supermacado'.

One year there were loads of cats around our apartment, we were later informed that kittens had been born in the wardrobe just weeks before we arrived! Mum was such an animal lover she simply had to feed them!

Growing up, Christmas was always great in our family. Mum's dinners were amazing, I still miss her gravy! We would go to midnight mass on Christmas Eve as Mum was very religious. Then on Christmas Day we would wake up to find that Santa had been! Stockings on our bed complete with satsuma! Then downstairs we would go to find the living room full of presents! We really were spoilt. Mum and Dad had this knack of making us feel like we were the luckiest kids in the world BUT then would always have your 'main' present to give to you after lunch, even though as a kid it felt like you had already had your 'main' present, it was amazing.

I remember being in the last year of school, so about 15 years old, when after lunch I could hear a mobile phone ringing. Now back in the day these were a rare commodity. I found the phone in the dining room, answered it and it was 'Father Christmas' (aka my cousins husband Ian) who told me that the phone was mine! WOW I was totally shocked and utterly grateful to Mum and Dad, but it was Mum who had arranged for the phone call to happen to make it even more special.

Mark Fielden   55

The Shrewsbury Flower Show was always a staple of the Fielden family diet as we were growing up, visiting year after year, the show dubbed the best flower show outside of Chelsea and the 'Worlds Wonder Show."

In my teenage years we would attend as members of the Shropshire Horticulture Society which would give you early access to the show and access to the members enclosure, Mum used to love going to the show, which took place over the second Friday and Saturday of August each year.

We would arrive early on the Friday, before the general public were allowed in, to view the various displays in the flower tents, the huge vegetables, and the jams and honeys that were being judged in the main competition tent. Mum really enjoyed this time of the morning on the opening show day, viewing the floral displays and tributes, but it was the amaryllis flowers that always caught her attention. We would follow up the early morning stroll around the tents with a coffee and then settle into the member's enclosure to watch the entertainment taking place in the main arena.

Mum particularly enjoyed watching the show jumping competitions, and was super excited when her favourite jumper Harvey Smith was taking part in the competition. Throughout the day we would to and fro from the members' enclosure around the show ground, visiting the many trade stalls and exhibitions that were taking place.

I remember having to visit the Klin stand on a yearly basis; this was a kitchen-based cleaner that would get dirt off literally anything! We would watch the demonstration and then purchase the cleaner at the special show price with lots of extras thrown in!

There was also the stand with the homemade crisps, they looked like pieces of plastic but when you put them in a deep fat fryer they turned into the most amazing tasting crisps. Just like the Klin, we watched the crisp demonstration every year as well and always ended up going home with a few bags at the end of the weekend! Early afternoon we would settle back into the members' enclosure ready to watch the entertainment in the main arena which culminated in the mass bands finale and grand firework display which was incredible.

The entertainment was fantastic, motorbike display teams, Household Calvary musical drive, parachutists; Dingle Fingle the clown, dog acrobatic displays, this show really had it all. My Uncle Peter, Mum's brother, was in the Shrewsbury Male Voice Choir and would perform alongside the marching military band in the build up to the musical finale and the fireworks.

Whilst the entertainment was going on, Mum, Dad and one of us kids used to head out of the showground to the nearby chip shop 'Roses' to get our tea and then buy a copy of the Sporting Pink on the way back in to catch up with all the days football results. Shrewsbury Town always played away from home on show day, so I remember being eager to see if they had won or not!

Looking back on the show, which still takes place every year today, I'm filled with so many happy memories of quality time and how much Mum used to love going along to it. On the Saturday evening when all the flower tents were closing the exhibitors would sell off their displays and flowers. Helen and Sally always timed this right to sneak off, returning later on with an amaryllis for Mum to take home after another successful and memorable weekend, leaving the showground after the fireworks to the sounds of the lone piper.

<u>4</u>

Fighting Spirit

Mum had been experiencing breathlessness and Dad kept asking her to see the GP. There were times when she was really struggling to breathe. However the older generation are often stoic and like to just get on with it, but I think she knew that there was something wrong, so she kept putting it off. I recall she had Quinsy once and refused to go to the GP then. Quinsy can be rather painful as it's an abscess that forms behind one of the tonsils caused by an infection. It actually got to the stage where it popped and her response was "See I'm fine", but that is how she was, very stubborn!

Mum did eventually go and see the GP about her breathing and was taken straight to A&E where they kept her in hospital. The test results showed that she had breast cancer and unfortunately it was quite advanced. Mum was diagnosed with breast cancer in 2015. Obviously getting such a diagnosis was a shock for everyone. Although there is no right or wrong way to feel after a diagnosis of breast cancer, our emotions went from fear, shock and anger to disbelief, sadness and numbness.

The days and weeks immediately after her diagnosis were particularly emotional and overwhelming. I had never dealt with anything like this before and pushed all my feelings down into the pit of my stomach to lessen the hurt. It felt like I had a big hole in my stomach and every morning when I got up it was still there.

Mum was offered chemotherapy, but she didn't want it, as she didn't want to lose her hair or for anyone else to know that she had cancer, not even her own sister. She was given medication to slow down the progress of the cancer but knew and accepted that this would not be a cure.

I remember getting a call from Dad in the middle of the night that Mum was really poorly and that he'd pick me up to go to the hospital. On arrival, I wasn't really sure what was going on; I was given a coffee and sat in a waiting room for what seemed like hours. Mum had taken a turn for the worse and had to be resuscitated during the night. This was a particularly scary time, I remember thinking 'how am I going to cope without her?'

It was after this she started her fight back. Unfortunately she had lost her voice due to damage caused when she had to be ventilated. It was difficult to understand her. She found it hard to speak and you could hardly hear what she was saying which really frustrated her, you had to really listen to make out her words, as saying 'pardon' meant she was using more energy to repeat herself. Mum was a real fighter; she had no help, but was determined to get her voice back. And over the weeks and months that followed, she did; of course she did! It was truly amazing to see, well, hear. It was unbelievable really.

Although Mum was really poorly, she fought hard to get well enough to be sent home. She was discharged with oxygen. However, Mum being Mum, she was not happy being reliant on oxygen, so she fought to get off it. She did too, which showed just how much determination she had. She was determined to carry on.

One afternoon she went for a walk in the town for a coffee with her sister Pat, she didn't want her to know that she was unwell. The main hill in the Town Centre where the shops are is called Pride Hill and its incline is not to be sniffed at. Mum walked it to see her sister at the coffee shop. I don't know how she managed it. To go from hospital and being on oxygen to then being able to walk around the town for a coffee without it was amazing. This sums up who she was and the strength she had.

Mum loved coffee, to her it was life. At home she would drink Camp coffee – this was her favourite. I remember once she took a bottle on holiday with her, only for Sally to drop it and see it smash on the floor whilst unpacking, after being in the apartment for less than an hour! Mum was gutted!

Mum began receiving support from the Lingen Davies treatment centre for regular check-ups. They created a treatment plan for her as part of the support. They were really great to Mum, to see their support was so humbling, even if it was just them doing their job, it meant a lot to us as a family.

When a parent is diagnosed with cancer, it can be an incredibly frightening time. The feelings of overwhelming shock and disbelief are followed by intense fear and worry. While there is no easy answer to the challenges that come with a cancer diagnosis, it is important to remember that there is hope and support available. Take time to process the diagnosis and take care of yourself; do not ignore your own needs.

5

The Void

It was St Patrick's Day 2017 and Mum was back in hospital. She was not very well but she was fairly stable. I had finished work so I went to visit her; I took my iPad with me as there were no TVs on the ward. Mum enjoyed watching sports, her passion was football, but she also enjoyed watching darts and snooker. We sat watching the Premier League match and chatting in between the action.

I remember her saying to me "You go, its St Patricks night. You go." There was an event on at The Inn on the Green pub.
"You go and have a beer and see your mates, I will be fine." I honestly don't know what stopped me going to the pub, especially as it was getting towards the end of visiting time, although we were allowed to stay a little later than the other visitors. I said no and stayed to watch the remainder of the game and the post-match reaction together. Mum was in the bed and I was sat on the chair next to her. As we watched the match she peppered it with her opinion of the game, as she always did, but little did I know then that this would be the last time we spoke, let alone watch football together.

The next day I was at work at Toys R Us when my sister called to say that Mum was really not well that morning. I don't remember her saying "Be prepared for the worst", only that she wasn't very well. I remember calling my area manager to ask if I couldn't get hold of him and if something happened, that could I leave. I was met with a voice at the other end of the phone saying "Bear with me." He was at a different store – he was at the Derby store with Dave who went on to become a big supporter of Chords Crush Cancer and was my best man at my wedding. It was the first time I had told my manager about Mum and he asked why I had not said anything before. I said that I was here to do my job, remaining professional by trying to keep work and private life separate and look after my family outside of the working environment. He was really supportive and said "Yeah of course."

A few hours later Sally rang me. She couldn't get her words out. I remember slumping back in the chair in my manager's office thinking 'Oh no.' between the sobs and the tears. She said "She's gone, she's gone, she's gone." I just started crying, letting all my emotion out; it's a phone call that I will never forget. I said I would get to the hospital as soon as I could.

I got off the phone and went outside to take some air and get my head around what I had been told. Mum's gone. It was such a huge thing to take in. This amazing woman who gave birth to you, brought you up, taught you right from wrong, spoilt you, loved you, cherished you was suddenly taken away. I felt as if the floor had given way under me. It was horrible. I tried to reach my area manager but couldn't get hold of him so I sent a text message. I called one of the other managers into the office and told him I was going off to the hospital. He didn't know what to say. On my way to the break room to collect my stuff, I popped into the toilet to wash my face and eyes as they were puffy. I had to walk through the store and I didn't want my staff to see their leader upset. I left and made my way to the hospital.

When I arrived at the hospital, I composed myself outside before going up to the ward. The end bed right by the window had the curtain drawn around it. My two sisters Helen and Sally were there as was my Dad. The atmosphere was heavy; it pushed down on me making it difficult to breathe. I looked at my sisters and Dad but couldn't say anything. Mum looked peaceful, not in any pain anymore, which was comforting. There was just a silence around the bed.

Everyone was sat with their thoughts and tears, saying nothing but the odd comment that would bring a smile, a memory. The staff brought us tea and biscuits. I guess drinking tea is what we do in these circumstances. I didn't really want one but I had one. I thought the hospital staff were excellent during those last moments. There was no rush to get us out. We could sit with her as long as we wanted to. We said our goodbyes one by one. I remember holding her hand, giving her a kiss and saying thank you for my life and her love and our family. As we left the room the nurses asked us about jewellery, whether or not we wanted it or should we leave it with Mum. I can't remember if we took it all, I think we left some but I know my sister Sally wanted some of it. It was one of those really difficult conversations. It was done nicely and compassionately.

I remember going back to Dads house to cook him a light meal of fish, chips and peas. Whilst I was taking the dog for a walk with Dad through one of the fields nearby, I thought 'what the hell is my dad going through?' Losing the woman he loved and had been with for so many years. Mum and Dad's bond was so close, they were inseparable. I was trying to look after Dad and make small chit chat about memories, but nothing can really take away the shock. I remember that dog walk being particularly awkward.

You're still in disbelief, the person's not there and what are you going to do without them? Mum was certainly the boss of our family! I cooked Dad his tea and then left him to his own peace so he could reflect in his own time. On my way home from Dads I actually went to the Inn on the Green and ordered a beer. I remember it was quite busy inside so I sat outside. It was a pretty cold evening but I still sat outside on one of the benches. I had a pint of Guinness and raised a glass to Mum and just sat in my own thoughts. One of the guys came over, one of the locals, and said "Are you okay, Mark?" he knew something was up. He left me to it and went inside. Craig the landlord came out with a beer and left it on the table and said "If you want to talk, I'm inside. If you don't want to, that's fine."

That evening, whilst I was sitting outside the pub Dave rang, "Are you okay bro?"
I said "No."
He said "Something's happened. Andy the area manager was with me today when you rang." I told him and he replied, "I am so sorry, if there is anything I can do."
That was really nice and reassuring, but what can people say in that moment? I didn't really know what to say back to him. It's comforting that they make a phone call even if it is full of silences. I will be forever grateful to Dave for making that call, it truly meant a lot to me.

Mark Fielden

Losing a parent to any form of cancer is an incredibly difficult experience, and breast cancer can be particularly challenging. It may be helpful to remember that you are not alone in this journey, as many others have experienced similar losses and understand what you're going through.

The loss of a parent is a deeply personal and unique journey, and its impact can be felt in various aspects of life; losing that connection can leave a void that is difficult to fill. Emotionally, the loss of a parent can lead to intense grief, sadness, and a profound sense of loss; feelings of emptiness, loneliness, and a longing for your parent's presence. It can also stir up a range of emotions such as anger, guilt, confusion, and even relief. Coping with these emotions takes time and can be a lifelong process. The loss of a parent can also have a significant impact on your identity and sense of self. Losing a parent can leave you feeling adrift and questioning your place in the world. It is a journey that is unique to each individual and requires compassion, understanding, and support from those around them. Remember that healing takes time, and there is no right or wrong way to grieve. It's okay to ask for help or support when you need it, and to take the time you need to heal and remember your parent in your own way.

I remember the first meeting we had with Father Edmund when planning Mum's funeral. It was at Dad's house and he was talking about aspects of the service. Mum was religious and an active church goer so we wanted a service that reflected that. It was held in the same church that Mum and Dad got married in. I remember him asking if anybody wanted to say some words on her life. I immediately said yes, almost without thinking about it. I had been the spokesperson for the family since her death and I wanted to stand and say a final goodbye on behalf of us all.

We selected some hymns in the time leading up to the funeral and a nice photo for the front of the Mass card. I spoke with Sally and Mum's sister Pat to get some background for what I wanted to say and then composed the speech, with many edits along the way, I wanted it to be perfect for Mum. Once I had completed it I read it out to Dad and Sally to make sure they approved. I then spent the next few days trying to learn it. I would read it out loud at home and when I was in the shower, trying to get confident that I knew the majority of the content so I was not always looking down at the pieces of paper, and also to manage my emotions.

On the morning of the funeral I read it aloud three, four, maybe five times to get it into my head before changing into my black suit and walking to Dad's house. Being in the house that day was surreal, everybody dressed in black, not quite knowing what to say, just waiting for the funeral cars to arrive to take us to the church.

Now I've never been in a limousine before, and I certainly did not want my first time to be in a funeral one, but here we were and off we went. Various neighbours made their way onto the street to say their own goodbye; nobody really spoke, just a nod of the head to let us know that they were thinking of us. The drive to the church was again very surreal. I noticed the amount of people who look at a funeral car as it passes by and remember feeling grateful to the other road users who would give way so that our car could keep behind in convoy of the car in front carrying Mum.

Arriving at the church, my cousin Dave, nephew Thomas, brother-in-law Chris and I carried the coffin into the church. It was heart-warming to see so many of Mum's church friends and our family members who had gathered to say goodbye. It was obviously a very sad moment but also a celebration of her life.

A strange moment for me, whilst so very sad it was a proud moment to take mum on her final journey, almost as If I was looking after her. As the service progressed, I remember becoming increasingly nervous and wanted to compose myself before my eulogy, I had tears rolling down my face during the hymn that proceeded myself speaking and the words I was trying to sing would just not come out.

Soon enough I was invited up onto the altar. I walked slowly past Mum's coffin, genuflected, and made my way to the lectern. I handed the priest a copy of my speech, he had suggested this in case I broke down and could not read my words, however, I was determined to not let this happen. I handed him the notes and took my place at the lectern, I remember taking a deep breath and then looking up.

Wow, the church was packed out. What a turn out for Mum, and all eyes were now on me. I spoke with passion and immense pride about Mum's life, who she was to us and others in the congregation who shared our love for her. I spoke about what a fantastic woman she was, a wonderful wife, mother, nan, sister and friend. I shared many memories and it was lovely to see people smiling, nodding, crying, and laughing with me as I spoke about Margaret, my Mum.

I got through the whole of the speech, of course I did, Mum guided me and gave me so much strength that day, I felt confident, proud and pleased that I had delivered the fitting send-off she truly deserved. As I made my way down from the altar I passed by the coffin, I touched the wood, said "Love you Mum," and then returned to my place in the pews.

It was without doubt the hardest thing I have ever had to do in my life. It was emotionally very difficult; we carried her into and out of the church for the service and then also carried her into the chapel at the crematorium. The crematorium was so much harder for me as I knew we would not be carrying her back out.

Eulogy

Good afternoon and thank you for joining us here today.

Margaret was born on 9th November 1941 here in Shrewsbury, Shropshire.

She grew up living at Brighton Terrace in Bradford Street with her mother Kathleen and was a younger sister to Bridget, Peter and Pat.

Attending the Cathedral School on Town Walls she was often home first whilst the rest of the family were out working, and it was her job to light the fire!!!

She took this role seriously and it actually led to a court appearance! She would count the coal bags into the shoot from the coal delivery and noticed that the coalman could not count as well as her! She reported this to her mother and celebrated victory in the courts.

Working life saw Margaret as a clerical assistant for Post Office Engineering based in Mardol which later moved to Telephone House.

She passed her time reading her book, until the supervisor came to check up on her, and had

Mark Fielden   73

extended breaks in the toilets to chat with her colleagues until getting caught and being told off!

Margaret met Tony at The Lion Hotel where every weekend there was 'Saturday night dancing'. He finally plucked up the courage to ask her for a drink to which she agreed. However, he had taken so much time in waiting to ask her, by the time they got to the bar it was closed!

Margaret and Tony married on 18th April 1970 in this very building, with a wedding reception held afterwards at The Shropshire Lad.

A wonderful caring mother to Helen, Sally and I, it was the grandchildren who were her pride and joy. She used to love watching Thomas and Kieran playing football and taking Lauren out for endless cups of coffee!!!

Over the years, Margaret alongside her housewife role where she cooked many a meal for the family and beyond, looked after many children as a childminder, a playschool assistant, a swimming club teacher and even helped out with school dinners when required. The kids used to love her doing this as she wouldn't force them to eat

everything on their plate – unlike the other dinner ladies!

She was actively involved with The Shrewsbury and District Stroke Club making pies, jam and of course her world-famous chocolate cake. I know many of you here today loved her chocolate cake and I've been told that she had a special way of cooking fish fingers too!

Margaret was a huge animal lover giving a home to dogs, cats and birds over the years. However, it was her first pet that was the most obscure. A tortoise called Michael.

Margaret loved her sport and started watching Shrewsbury Town play from an early age. She spoke about the talent of Arthur Rowley and in later life if there was football on the telly then she would be watching it! She was also into her Darts, cheering on her favourite Barney and always hoping that Phil Taylor would miss his next shot!

After the church we had a small service at the crematorium followed by light refreshments at The Inn on the Green.

6

Sally

Growing up, our childhood was a very happy one. I particularly loved our family holidays, my earliest memory is sitting on Mum's knee on a beach in Anglesey; she was telling me off for rubbing sand off my hands all over her. I have the photo of this as a screen saver on my phone which makes me smile every day.

Our holidays abroad were the best; we always had a villa with a pool. Mum trying to get on the li-lo was hilarious, tipping off it time and time again; she was determined though and eventually succeeded to a round of applause.

Christmas was also a very special time, she loved entertaining, cooking Christmas dinner for everyone and making sure we all had lots of presents. She loved spoiling everyone, especially the grandchildren when they came along.

Mum was our "Olympus Lady" – she was given this name as she had a pair of Olympus trainers, if it was windy we called her "Olympus Lady Windswept" as she had very thick hair which got very messy when blown about in the wind. She was strong, loving, warm and caring, with a cracking sense of humour, she loved spending time with her family and friends and helping others whenever she could.

She was always happy to help out at fundraising events raising money for Stroke Club, Axis, Marks football teams raising funds to buy the kit, the Church, and school events. I think this must be where Mark gets his fundraising skills from, raising valuable funds to help others.

A cancer diagnosis is a devastating blow for anyone to experience, but when you find out your mum has cancer, your whole world gets turned upside down. It's important to try to stay positive and hopeful, and not feel guilty about telling her wonderful news about your own life; after all, she wants you to be happy.

One of the most difficult things about supporting another person through cancer treatment is respecting their choices. Whether it's choosing to undergo treatment or not, we don't always agree with the path that our loved one takes. Whether or not you agree it's important to respect their wishes and provide them with what they need most of all right now, your unconditional love.

I was always kept up to date with Mum's hospital appointments and her blood results, she always came back very happy when her levels came back low. I helped with the administration of her tablets and checking her oxygen levels with her. Apart from that, I just spent time with her, taking her shopping, making sure we had a coffee or two as you could never go into town without stopping for coffee! I would watch football with her, which was another love of her life, and doing jigsaw puzzles.

I had to attempt to cut her hair which had got very thin due to the tablets she was on and she didn't want to go to the hairdressers as they would know she had been ill. Her hair did eventually grow back thick so I could hang up my scissors and razor. Thank goodness as hairdressing isn't really my thing!

Whilst Mum was battling with cancer it was very much business as usual, she was determined to keep everything as normal as possible for the sake of the grandchildren. She continued to look after them, take them out and cook for us all, she was truly amazing.

The day Mum passed away was the worst day of my life. I had gone to the hospital in the morning as we were allowed to visit whenever we wanted to. When I arrived I put Mum's clean nighties in the cupboard and sat by her bed, she was talking a little but seemed agitated. She wanted me to take her to the toilet, I asked one of the nurses and he said he would come over. She grabbed my arm and said quite firmly "NO, you take me". She then slumped over and I had to hold her up until the nurse came over to help.

They made her comfortable then got the doctor over to speak with her. The doctor spoke about operating to which she clearly replied "No operation." I was then asked to go to a room to speak to the doctor. She said that she was poorly and may not survive an operation, I asked if I should call the family to come in and she said that there was no immediate rush. I phoned Dad, Helen & Mark to update them.

Dad and Helen arrived at the hospital and we sat around Mum's bed. She was awake but wasn't talking, I distinctively remember her holding on to and playing with the cross she always wore around her neck.

Mark Fielden   79

She was peaceful and I just sat watching her chest rising up and down as she breathed. I can't remember how long we were sat there, possibly an hour or so it didn't seem that long when I noticed her breathing was slowing down, her chest stopped going up and down. I looked over at Helen and said she's stopped breathing. I went to get the nurse, and then the doctor came in and confirmed she had gone.

I remember shouting "NO" and the tears started to fall. She was gone. She went peacefully, my only regret was not being able to get Mark there in time, but in the end it was very quick.

When Mark started his fundraising journey I think it was just supposed to be a one off event. Due to the popularity and success of the first event he decided to hold a 2nd, bigger and better than the first and here we are now heading towards the 8th event! It is a great achievement providing vital funds for the valuable work of the Lingen Davies team.

It was great when Mark said he wanted to start raising money for Lingen Davies, the hardest part was convincing Mum that he wasn't doing it because of her illness. She kept asking me "He's not doing this because of me is he?" Sorry Mum if I told a little white lie!

I have attended every Chords Crush Cancer event. I have helped out with everything that Mark has asked me to do in order to help make the night a success. That has included selling and folding the hundreds of raffle tickets. I also buy a helium balloon every year with a photo of Mum printed on it so that she is always with us on the night. If Mum was here now she would still be helping fold raffle tickets for the event and helping Mark come up with new fundraising ideas, she was very supportive and had a way of getting people to part with their money. She would be proud of everything he has achieved (As long as he wasn't doing it because of her!!)

Mark, AKA little bro, what can I say....... I am immensely proud of everything that you have achieved in raising over £19,000.00 for Lingen Davies Cancer Fund, this goes towards buying vital equipment to help the treatment of cancer patients throughout the community. The hours of your own time you put into this event every year to help others is remarkable. Keep up the good work and go smash the £20,000.00 at CCC8 in 2024.

Mark Fielden   81

7

Chords Crush Cancer

Coping with the loss of a parent can be one of the most traumatic experiences a person can have. The pain and sorrow can be overwhelming and it can take time to come to terms with the loss. It is important to allow yourself to grieve in whatever way works best for you, whether it's crying, talking to friends and family, or participating in activities that help you remember the good times. It is also important to take care of yourself physically and emotionally by eating healthy, getting enough rest, and avoiding unhealthy coping mechanisms such as alcohol or drugs. Finding a support system and talking to someone who can provide understanding and compassion can also be helpful. It takes time, but in time you will learn to adapt and come to live with your loss.

Following the support and advice that Lingen Davies had given not only to Mum but to me and the family too, I wanted to find a way to say thank you. I knew the way forward would be to fundraise. After all if I could continue to help others in Mums memory that is what I would do. I spoke to my family about it and they all agreed that it was a good idea and were fully on board.

Fundraising is an essential aspect of any non-profit organization or charitable cause. It is the process of gathering financial support from individuals, corporations, or foundations to sustain and further the mission of the organization. However, fundraising is not without its challenges. One of the primary challenges of fundraising is the increasing competition for limited resources. With numerous non-profits and charitable causes vying for the same pool of donors, it can be challenging to stand out. Donors are often bombarded with requests for support, making it difficult for fundraisers to capture their attention and convince them to contribute.

Fundraising is a noble endeavour that brings immense satisfaction to those who engage in it. While the primary goal of fundraising is to generate financial support, the satisfaction derived from this activity goes far beyond monetary gains. One of the most fulfilling aspects of fundraising is the opportunity to make a positive impact on society. Whether it is for a charitable organization, a community project, or a social cause, fundraising allows individuals to contribute to something greater than themselves. By actively participating in fundraising efforts, individuals can witness first-hand the difference their contributions make in the lives of others. This sense of fulfilment stems from the knowledge that their efforts are directly improving the lives of others.

It's hard to know what will motivate people to donate to charity so I knew that whatever I did was going to have to be different to what is already out there but also fun. As Lingen Davies is based in Shrewsbury and we are from there too it seemed only right to host the event locally, so where else than in a pub? Knowing that I was going to host the event in a pub, just not which one yet, I had to think "outside of the box." I did however know that I wanted to include music.

Music has always been a powerful tool for bringing people together, evoking emotions, and creating a sense of unity. It is no wonder that music has found its way into the world of fundraising, where its ability to captivate and inspire has been harnessed to raise funds for various causes. The use of music in fundraising events has proven to be an effective strategy, not only in generating financial support but also in creating awareness and fostering a sense of community. One of the primary reasons why music is so effective in fundraising is its universal appeal. Regardless of age, gender, or cultural background, music has the ability to resonate with people on a deep emotional level. It has the power to evoke feelings of joy, sadness, nostalgia, and hope.

In 2016 I was working at Toys R Us. Christmas was out of the way, however in retail nothing really stops, and it was on to the annual inventory. This often happens around my birthday so I never get the chance to celebrate as we are working 12 hour shifts most days in the run up to the stock take and working many late evenings. It was a typical January evening, cold and dark, and damp that hung in the air. I decided to stop off at The Inn on the Green pub in Radbrook on my way home from work. The warmth of the bar felt good on my face as I went in out of the cold. The bar wasn't busy as it was a Monday evening, and the darts team who usually play there on a Monday were away from home. I sat myself in my usual spot at the end of the dark oak bar that I was familiar with milling, over the beers and bottles on display.

The Inn on the Green is a typical local pub with a community feel to it, I guess it's the typical community local that serves the people of Radbrook Green. The pub has a football team and dominos and darts teams that play from there. It serves good food at a reasonable price and does a lovely Sunday lunch. The pub has been fully renovated in recent years so it looks a lot different these days to what it did at our first event.

Mark Fielden   85

Whilst propping up the bar that evening, I was enjoying my usual pint of Guinness and talking to Craig, the landlord, about my idea. Craig was a youngish local taking on his first pub; he did a good job in uniting the local community and became a good friend, somebody who was not just a landlord but somebody who you could chat to and bounce ideas off. Craig had previously done some fundraising in his pub for Lingen Davies, so I wanted to pick his brain for ideas of what had worked and not worked in his experience.

We spent a good hour, hour and a half, batting around ideas and potential names. I wanted to come up with a name that included the word cancer as I felt that had to be part of it. I was texting my musical friends when Ian, who also worked at the pub, joined our discussion. I had the idea of asking some musician friends to perform on the night and what we might call the event.

The ideas were flowing around; 'Chords, Help You,' was one, as it reflected the musical side I was after. With much scribbling on pieces of paper and looking for glimmers of inspiration, Ian eventually came up with the name Chords Crush Cancer; playing on the musical word chords aiming to crush the cancer.

The name was unique and rolled off the tongue so was easily memorable whilst reflecting the theme of the event. It was perfect! I chose to host the event in the February, as the first Saturday in February is world cancer day and thought it would be apt.

World Cancer Day is led by the UICC, the Union for International Cancer Control. It is one singular initiative under which the entire world can unite together in the fight against the global cancer epidemic. The aim is to raise worldwide awareness, improve education and motivate personal, collective and government action to re-imagine a world where millions of preventable cancer deaths are saved and access to life-saving cancer treatment and care is non-discriminatory for all.

Since its inception in 2000, World Cancer Day has grown into a positive movement to face one of our greatest challenges in history. Each year, hundreds of activities and events take place around the world, gathering communities, organisations and individuals in schools, businesses, hospitals, marketplaces, parks, community halls, places of worship - in the streets and online - acting as a powerful reminder that we all have a role to play in reducing the global impact of cancer.

While we live in a time of inspirational advancements in cancer prevention, diagnosis and treatment, many of those suffering and seeking cancer care can experience barriers at every turn. Income, education, geographical location and discrimination based on ethnicity, gender, sexual orientation, age, disability and lifestyle are just a few of the factors that can negatively impact care.

Getting the ball rolling was mainly me although Craig helped me sell raffle tickets at the pub. I set up a Just Giving page for those who could not make the evening. I really didn't have any experience of fundraising, but it was exhilarating! Given it was January and the event was to be held in February I'd not given myself much time to plan!

I was excited to raise some money for Lingen Davies after Mum's diagnosis and I just threw everything at it; anything I thought would help to make a good event. I was amazed at the amount of people that came along. I was often in the pub as it's a local, popping in for a drink or a meal after work. The way the local community rallied around for the first event was first class and I was very grateful.

I contacted my friend Davy Lewis, a musician who was playing the Temple Bar circuit in Ireland. When it comes to nightlife Temple Bar is the most famous place in Dublin, for tourists and locals. Temple Bar is now promoted as Dublin's cultural quarter, and thanks to its bustling nightlife it has become famous with tourists around the world. During the 18th century, it was THE place to go if you were looking for a sex worker after a night of drunken depravity. As the years went by, the area became worse and this resulted in bargain rents for homes, boutiques and bars. The area quickly became a hub of Irish bohemian peculiarity – like in Soho in London – and as the locals started to like it, it became a trendy neighbourhood. The Irish Government decided to modernise and rejuvenate the area in 1991, making it even more popular.

I first met Davy during my first visit to Dublin, I was there for a couple of nights, and being a typical tourist, I wanted to check out the famous Temple Bar pub. I remember the place being rammed, there were live music acts performing throughout the day and I guess I arrived just at the right time.

Davy's voice was incredible and I really enjoyed his set, whilst soaking up the atmosphere in the home city of my favourite beer! Pint of Guinness in hand, I stood and watched his performance, smiling, jigging and singing along as he belted out tune after tune. I managed to grab a quick word with him after his set to say how much I enjoyed it; it was very brief as he was dashing off to the next pub for his next gig.

The next evening after having a meal in The Quays restaurant, I walked outside towards the Liffey River and heard the unmistakeable voice from the night before. Where was it coming from? I knew that I'd like to watch him perform again. I followed the sounds and ended up at The Merchants Arch, a wonderful pub right opposite the famous H'apeny Bridge. I went inside, grabbed a Guinness and looked for a seat; I managed to find one to the left of the stage area.

I'm not sure if he had recognised me from the night before, as playing three to four gigs a day I'm sure that he had many people who enjoyed his music that would want to talk to him, but we exchanged a nod of heads in between songs and I was having a really lovely evening.

I managed to grab a quick chat with him outside during a break in his set, and then as he was coming towards the end of his show he threw one of his CD's across the room to me with a cheeky smile. On returning home from Ireland, I listened to the CD and made contact with him via Facebook. I was not sure if I would get a response or not but sure enough I did, and our friendship grew from there.

He got me involved with his social media presence. I created a website to share his live performances with his fans. Davy had set up a European tour and had his debut album released just in time for his departure. He shipped me about 200 copies that I could use for promo; I really didn't know he was sending that many, so it was a real surprise when they arrived at my parents' house!

I was living with Mum and Dad at the time, and I remember Mum's face thinking *'what on earth has just been delivered?!'* I put the album on straight away. I was delighted to be one of the first to hear his new music, and Mum seemed to enjoy it too.

Over the years I visited Dublin many times to watch Davy play, often staying at his house, we would travel into the city centre for up to three gigs a day. I would sit at the bar with my favourite Guinness and listen to him belting out the tunes. There is generally live music on from midday each day right the way through until the early hours of the morning.

I remember heading to the Merchants Arch for an afternoon set before having some chill time before the next gig at 11pm in The Norseman. Crazy stuff! The one memory that sticks out is an afternoon gig in The Quays Bar. We had arrived and Davy was all set up, we sat at the bar sharing a few stories over a beer and the bar was really quiet, but Dublin pubs really are something else! About 20 minutes or so into his set a hen party arrived and really took to his music, singing along and building a really fun atmosphere inside the pub. The music and energy must have travelled onto the street, as by halfway through his set the place was bouncing.

I remember taking some footage for his social media pages during the final few songs; he really did have the crowd eating from the palm of his hand. From such a quiet start to an afternoon set, to a full pub in full voice was simply something to behold, I had to remind myself that this was a weekday afternoon and not kicking out time on a Saturday night!

It was a gig that I will never forget. Davy spent a couple of summers in Greece which was great fun. I'd travel to Tsilivi for a week at a time to meet up with him and watch him perform in the evenings. We would spend the day chilling by the pool or playing pool and mini golf, although he always used to beat me, and then we would grab a bite to eat before heading to Molly Malone's for his evening sessions. He would play for hours and really drew in the crowds, enjoying their holiday evenings with drinks and live music.

He said that he would fly over for the event which was a real coup for me. Davy came up with the idea of having a request set for the evening, comprising of a song sheet with over 150 songs to be distributed around the pub that people could choose from and when he sung their chosen song they could make a contribution. It went down rather well.

Over the years I built up a really good friendship with Davy, I was an usher at his beautiful wedding to Mandy which was held in South Africa, and travelled with him to Oslo and Washington DC to fulfil music bookings in Irish bars overseas. Davy played Carly down the aisle at our wedding which was such a lovely touch and has been a huge supporter of Chords Crush Cancer.

Mark Fielden   93

After event impromptu acoustic sessions sat at the bar at the Inn on the Green, and also back at my house, are personal favourites and memories that I will cherish.

I also spoke to my other musician friends Rob Cooper and Si Davies of Cooper & Davies. Cooper & Davies came together through a desire to play roots Americana in a style of their own drawing on the traditions of country and blues, with a modern alternative-indie sound. They were chosen to play on the BBC Introducing Stage at The Long Road Festival in 2018, then later that year Cooper & Davies played The Saloon Stage at the huge Country to Country (C2C) Festival at The O2. C2C is a country music festival that has been held in Europe every year since 2013 and has had the likes of Keith Urban, Lady Antebellum, Dixie Chicks and The Shires perform. Cooper & Davies also agreed to play at my Chords Crush Cancer event.

I first met Rob Cooper and Simon Davies, from the duo Cooper & Davies, whilst on a night out in Bridgnorth. They were playing at The Bear pub and I recall it being a fantastic evening. I love listening to live music, having done so in and around my hometown of Shrewsbury since my late teens. I remember being struck by their style of music, and knew that I wanted to see them play again. In the months that followed they had some gigs in Shrewsbury so I made sure that I was there!

They played at The Old Post Office, The Wheatsheaf and The Kings Head. It was after one of the gigs at The Old Post Office that I got chatting to them both and over the months that followed struck up a strong friendship with them. I would meet them at gigs and they would ask me to get them a beer when they were playing. I had to make sure that I didn't spill on their equipment when arriving on stage, after collecting their drinks from the bar! I remember it being quite surreal on a couple of occasions when people in the audience would look at me wondering why I was delivering the band their beers!

Mark Fielden   95

It certainly struck up a number of conversations with the crowds and enabled me to share the band info and add more people to the growing social media fan base! After a couple of years of following them they asked me if I would design them a website, which I did, and they added me to their social media accounts so that I could post updates for the band.

I've been interested in social media for a few years, so it was a real honour to be asked to support them in this way. Over the years we became really good friends, meeting up in Shrewsbury or their hometown of Bridgnorth for drinks, I was invited to both of their weddings and Rob was an usher at my own wedding in April 2023. I travelled with them to Farmer Phil's Festival, to Theatre Severn and Ludlow when they supported Quill and to Birmingham and Lemington Spa when they were asked to support CC Smugglers.

The highlight for me however was travelling with the band to the Country to Country Festival at the O2 in London. The band, myself and their families travelled down on a minibus to watch them perform, I had organised t-shirts with the band logo for us all to wear to support them, and as I was on website and social media duties, I went backstage into the greenroom to share a beer with them whilst they sound checked which was an amazing experience.

Rob and Si played at my surprise 40th birthday party organised by Carly, have been huge supporters of Chords Crush Cancer and even played at our wedding. Who would have thought that a night out in Bridgnorth to watch some live music would lead to such great friendships with two really cracking blokes?!

To have these two quality acts for the event was just amazing. To have a strong calibre of musicians was a real positive start. I knew that the music would be first class and people who turned up would love watching them play.

Rob Cooper, who plays bass, harmonica and sings in Cooper & Davies, first met me in 2011 at The Bear in Bridgnorth. "As a fan of live music Mark would often be at our gigs and he has supported us a lot over the years. I first heard about CCC when Mark approached me with the idea asking if I'd help him choose a name for the event and if we'd play at it. We play up beat Americana music. Harmony based old time songs."

Cooper & Davies performed at the first event, and at every one since, excluding the cancelled event in 2021 because of the pandemic. "I continued to support the event because it's always a good night and a great fundraiser for a local charity that does really important work. Mark has great strengths as an event organiser. He's persistent in getting hold of quality prizes for the fundraiser and he has a great social media presence to raise awareness. He also adds the personal touch of how his mother inspires him to work hard on the event, her memory and how he pays tribute really comes across."

"Every year I have a tradition of texting Mark 10 minutes before I arrive saying I can't make it as the speakers have blown up or something. I did this on the first year which caused Mark to panic but he had great relief when we all walked through the door minutes later. I now text him every time to remind him of the joke."

I was blown away by the quality of music on the night too and more so as the local music scene back then was not huge. People who came on the evening asked me who the acts were, a couple of them wanted to purchase CD's of the original music which we accommodated at our 2nd event. The music really was first class and I was delighted that so many people were asking about my friends and when they would be playing in Shrewsbury again!

In addition to the music performances, I decided to host a raffle and an auction, so we needed some prizes. I contacted local friends, family and businesses but I didn't really know where to start. I looked on Google how to get prizes for a fundraising event and eventually ended up with 80!

Not a bad start. When I look back at the raffle prizes I don't think they were that great as they included a PlayStation game, an Xbox game and a bottle of wine, but it was a start, it got us up and running. In terms of the auction, I got in touch with a few local companies; we managed to get a signed Shrewsbury Town football shirt signed by the players, we had a ukulele donated and we managed to get hold of an acoustic guitar from a local music shop. Minecraft figures from the game were really popular at the time too. A guy called TDM was doing signings and we managed to get a figure of him autographed. Daniel Robert Middleton, better known online as DanTDM, is an English YouTuber, author, and gamer known best for his video game commentaries including Minecraft, Roblox, Pokémon and Sonic the Hedgehog, along with other content.

I knew that to get as many people to the event as possible, that I would have to promote it, so I thought that I had better contact the local newspapers. I had some success and made it into the press. I even managed three paragraphs in the Shrewsbury Chronicle. I knew that I had to get online to promote the event too. We spend an average of 2.5 hours a day on social networks and messaging; so social media is an important part of our daily lives. Social media is a fast way to get news out about the event and it was better than

Mark Fielden   99

having to go door to door with flyers. Having a social page also helped to get and grow followers of those interested and likely to come and support the event.

Although I wasn't great on social media then, I did set up a Facebook event page and had a go at tweeting. My efforts were rewarded when I had responses to my tweets, and people signing up to the event page to say they were coming. A friend of mine from school, Adam, had set up his own business, APT Photography, as a photographer and took photos of the evening for us free of charge. The pictures were great and could be added to Facebook and Twitter to showcase the event. Looking back now there are some really great photos that bring back memories of a really enjoyable first evening.

On the night I was nervous about how successful the event would be, so I immersed myself with making sure things went to plan after such a lot of preparation. The evening was going swimmingly until the landlord's brother called me on stage to say a few words. I was not prepared at all. I didn't know what to say as I had not prepared a speech. I was not composed, and I was stuttering from nerves to the point that I nearly dropped my phone on the floor when I was referring to it to look at who I should thank! I certainly didn't imagine that the event would be so popular, nor did I think that I would need to say anything other than 'thank you for coming.'

Mark Fielden

8

Strike Whilst the Iron is Hot

The first event raised over £1100 pounds; I was certainly not expecting to get anywhere near that. I don't know what I was really expecting other than hoping to achieve £500 and any more would be a massive bonus. Looking back, its a million miles away from what we currently achieve given that we now have some experience of hosting fundraising events.

Davy and his girlfriend Mandy were staying with me, so the next day we went into town to get some breakfast at The Loopy Shrew restaurant in the Town centre – we never actually ate anything though as our food never arrived! So it was just a coffee and an OJ, before rushing to get them both to the station before their train departed for Birmingham International, so that they could catch their flight back to Ireland. After dropping them both at the station and thanking them for their support and wishing them a safe journey, I called in to The Boathouse Pub. The Boathouse is one of Shrewsbury's most loved historic pubs. Its stunning location on the banks of the River Severn gives it magnificent views of the river and the Quarry Park.

I sat inside the old pub looking out of the window at the walking suspension bridge with a pint of my favourite Guinness in hand thinking about the night before and what I had actually achieved – I had hosted my first fundraising event which had been a huge success.

That afternoon after a brief visit to my house to recharge my phone, I called into the Inn on the Green to thank Craig. There were people in there who were in the night before, and they all told me 'Wow, what a fantastic event last night was. Are you doing it again next year? It needs to be an annual event.' That planted the seed in my mind to do more. It took me some time to reflect on the evening and its success, and to think about what I had learnt and what could be done better. I did however, feel extremely proud and very excited about the adventure I was about to embark on.

It was important to strike whilst the iron was hot so to get the ball rolling; I launched our official Chords Crush Cancer Facebook page on 1st March 2015. I launched the events page with a small video I created from images of the first event and what to expect at the second, and it quickly gained a small following from those who had been at the first event.

The day after I launched the event page there was a post from a guy called Robbie Wheelan who is a friend of Davy's; he's known locally as 'The Mayor of Temple Bar' and is a huge character in and around Dublin. He posted 'flights booked' so I was super excited that he was coming to the second event. Davy agreed to play again as did Cooper & Davies so I was grateful to them. It felt as if things were starting to naturally progress.

We launched the official poster for the event on 18th Jan 2016, looking back at it now it was a bit cringe but back then my Microsoft Word skills were very limited. We also managed to gain press coverage again, I started tweeting and followed up with a couple of journalists. Lisa O'Brien, who was the chief reporter at The Shropshire Star at the time, very kindly wrote an interview about me and Chords Crush Cancer.

I know that wrist bands are always popular with music festival goers so I thought it would be nice to have some for the next event. I contacted a company called PAC wrist bands; they were helpful and generous and supplied us with Chords Crush Cancer branded bands. We launched them on the Facebook page for a donation. These bands are a rare thing now so you're lucky if you have one.

We also had branded Chords Crush Cancer T-shirts made. The design was a vinyl record with the Chords Crush Cancer words on it. I still have one that I use for promotion photographs given it was the first t-shirt we produced.

I found myself fully in the flow of doing social media and beginning to get into the habit of messaging companies over Facebook messenger and using the occasional Tweet; this is when our prize journey really began to take off, we were able to secure some really good prizes for the auction. The donations included another signed Shrewsbury Town shirt and a signed football, a signed Everton first team print in a frame, and a £200 ferry voucher from Brittany Ferries. Davy was making his own ukuleles and electric guitars out of old oil cans and they looked absolutely fantastic so he donated one of those to us, and he played it on the evening too. The top prize had to be the one from Manchester United Football Club. I contacted the Manchester United Foundation to see if they were willing to donate a prize. I was put into a draw along with other charities and organisations, if you're lucky to get chosen you get a signed prize. I was really lucky and received a signed football. On the night of the event we had a married couple actually bidding against each other for the Manchester United signed football, complete with certificate of authenticity!

We were finally off the starting block for achieving good quality prizes. Jail House tours also became involved. Shrewsbury Prison was an active prison until it was decommissioned in 2013 by the government and the tours took over. Led by an ex-prison officer who shines light on what life was like for prisoners, the tour brings the prison to life through a no-holds-barred experience. Shrewsbury Prison is also known to be the second most haunted jail in the world and visitors can visit and investigate what lurks behind the high prison walls in the dead of night with ghost tours. The fun doesn't end there either; visitors can even try to do a jail break! We also had tickets from Chester Racecourse donated so the winner could attend one of their exhilarating races.

This event was coming together nicely but I wanted to inject more into it and thought having comedians on board could be a good move. I approached a company called Comedy Loft who donated tickets to one of their shows. Comedy Loft deliver four different acts at every show, including some of the best up & coming comperes and headliners from the UK & abroad. Before the show starts guests enjoy tasty delights and have a drink and chat with friends. Once the comedy show has ended there is an after show party where guests get to wine, dine, laugh some more and dance!

The night itself was brilliant. Davy did another request set and Cooper & Davies sang their usual set-list of feel good songs that get you toe tapping and dancing along. Robbie Wheelan joined Davy pelting out a couple of songs. Robbie is not a singer but loves Karaoke and certainly got the ladies up dancing! There was a real Irish atmosphere to the room. Robbie has joined us a few times since. Also making their debut at the second event were my close friends Dave and Andrea. I knew Dave from my Toys R Us days and he was also my best man at my wedding. They pitched in selling raffle tickets, name the bear, t-shirts – basically anything that they could do to help and really bought into the event.

I can certainly say that the second event provided many lessons in fundraising, although I was still learning on the hoof, the whole evening was much more professional and the prizes far superior to the first. Having my family on board supporting me helped to take the load and having Mum there selling raffle tickets was wonderful. Sadly we didn't know that this would be Mums last event.

9

Carly

Carly and I first met in 1999/2000 at Walford College. "We had a mutual friend at the time and would hang out together at breaks and lunch. Mark takes great pride in the fact that he paid for a packet of Frazzles from the vending machine for me and Mark being Mark he even managed to incorporate it into his wedding speech!"

"Even though we were at the same college, we had very different lives as we were studying different courses and we lost touch, although we would always say hi if we bumped into each other. We would occasionally cross paths over the years as I would visit his store Toys R Us, as I have triplets so was always in there. We would see Mark walking up and down the aisles and would always say hello.

In 2017 Carly became single, and as a busy working mum to three seven-year-olds she didn't really have time for dating, and it wasn't something she was looking to pursue. "A friend persuaded me to give Tinder a try, and I thought *'well I have nothing to lose, why not'*. After a short time, I got rid of the app as dating was a mine field and I didn't just have me to think about."

"In the September I decided to give the app another try; I swiped left and right accordingly then who should appear on my screen but Marks profile. I instantly recognised him, smiled to myself, a familiar face, who I knew was a true and real profile, and gave him a swipe right."

"Mark often reminds me he gave me a super-like, something I didn't even know you could do. We chatted a while through the app and as fate would have it we both had the day off so we met for a drink. It was easy as I knew this guy. Even if I didn't know him well, it was easy and natural to talk to Mark, I knew I could trust him and he was a genuine good guy."

"We met after CCC2. Mark had never spoken about CCC or his mum's death before as he felt that they were something that should be discussed face to face. This reinforced my thoughts of 'this is a good guy'. I loved and still love listening to Mark talking about his fundraising, and you can tell it means so much to him as it's evident in everything he does and says. He is always so excited and will proudly chat for hours to anyone who will listen."

"When Mark first told me about his events I didn't know how our relationship would unfold but I knew I wanted to support him in it. Having worked in a local hospice I have seen first-hand what cancer does to families and I know Marks love for his mum is at the forefront of what he does. I decided then that after our first date, whatever happened afterwards, I would go to his next event."

"We met at the Boathouse in Shrewsbury on September 4th 2017. Mark was hoping to walk to the Boathouse for our date and I happened to drive past. I stopped to give him a lift. He didn't really want me to give him a lift but I did anyway. We got to the Boathouse and I remember feeling the safest I had felt in a long time in his company. We talked, laughed and even cried when he was telling me about his mum. It was so natural, not forced. In the early days not once did I question what I was doing, was this right, what about the kids I knew he was the one I could spend the rest of my life with and six years later here we are."

"Mark had asked me to be his girlfriend before the next event came and our relationship was growing by the day, and by the time the event came I was really proud to be part of something so incredible. In a way I feel closer to his mum through these events, even though I never met her as she is sadly no longer with us. I was not sure what to expect of the events but they are more of a success than I imagined."

Mark and Carly with comedian Jethro

Chords Crush Cancer 1st Event

Simon Davies, Davy Lewis, Rob Cooper and Mark

Mark's First Speech

Davy Lewis

Mark Fielden   113

Auction

Davy Lewis

Chords Crush Cancer 2nd Event

Mark thumbs up

Aunty Pat and Dad

Lone Dancer

Manchester United signed football

Mark Fielden

Chords Crush Cancer 3rd Event

Mark and Carly selfie frame

Name the Bear

Mark Fielden   121

Window Art

Chords Crush Cancer 4th Event

Mark and Carly roller banner

Mark Fielden

Mark and Mums balloon

Dublin Crew

Davy Lewis

Dave & Andrea – T-shirt sellers

Mark Fielden   127

Dublin Group photo

Memories of Margaret

10

Third Time Lucky

After the success of the second event, sadly Mum deteriorated and passed away. During the months after her funeral, I discussed with my father Tony and my sisters Helen and Sally whether I should continue raising funds in her memory. The overwhelming answer was a firm yes.

I was committed to delivering a third event but it had some stumbling blocks on the way. The Inn on the Green had been such a great host to us for events one and two but Craig the landlord had left the pub and gone onto pastures new. I had a brief discussion with the new landlady and landlord, but with them being new at the time and trying to settle in, I didn't think it was fair on them so made the decision to move the event to another local pub called The Red Barn. I knew the landlord and lady there and knew the venue would be big enough; they were very welcoming and agreed to us holding our third event in their pub. The Red Barn is a fantastic, Cask Marque accredited pub just outside Shrewsbury town centre. Being right at the heart of the local community, it was a great location for the event.

Having secured the pub, I decided to do something slightly different. I was aware that the first two events had the same musicians and although they are very talented and good friends of mine I wanted to mix it up a bit. An ex-work colleague of mine at Toys R Us and local musician Andy Mills agreed to join the line-up.

Andy Mills is a solo act with an acoustic guitar and a microphone, often covering songs from full bands. "I don't tend to do that thing where you try and play a more gentle or sympathetic version of the song just because it's on an acoustic guitar and I'm on my own. I usually give it a lot of energy and play with a good amount of conviction which hopefully shines through and gets people in the mood for dancing or joining in singing" he said. "I don't like to be too genre based in the type of songs I play as I feel that if you've got a mixed audience in a venue such as a pub on a Saturday night, then I think variety is key. I could go from Bo Diddley, to Cher, to Neil Young, to MGMT, to Haircut 100 or Tom Waits or The Who. As for playing my original music, it depends if people make a particular point about wanting to hear it."

Andy first met Mark when he started working at Toys R Us around 18 years ago. "When I left there I hadn't seen him in a very long time but within the last few years we started bumping into each other at a couple of pubs and got talking again. Things picked up from there really regarding the music and participating in the yearly CCC Charity event. I think I've done 4 of them now."

"Mark first approached me after a gig at The Inn on The Green, Radbrook. I was happy to do it as it's a fantastic cause to support, a great way to generate a good donation of money to Lingen Davies and the fact that Mark and Carly, and all of the other people involved genuinely give this event their all. It's so very well supported and they spend a lot of the year enquiring about charity donations for things like raffles, auctions and the music is well organized with a good layout of times for people to play. It's just a superb night to be involved with. I feel like I've committed to it and there's no reason why I wouldn't continue to support this event as it's a really enjoyable, social evening for a worthy cause."

Mark Fielden   131

"Mark's determination and organization for the event are certainly strengths. If he's been phoning, emailing and writing to people such as comedians, football teams, TV personalities etc. and asking for any support in the way of donations then I'm sure he's had a fair few occasions where he's been ignored or knocked back; but he continues to not be disheartened by it and just focuses on the goal at the end which is to generate a decent night, with a good selection of quality prizes in order to raise the greatest amount of money for the charity. CCC always runs smoothly and everybody in the pub has a great night out so it's really fun to support."

Mills has seen the event grow year on year and the attendance increases along with the money rising each time. "I hope it continues to do so as it's clearly a successful night with a lot of support behind it. One year I entered the raffle but had to leave early. I forgot that I'd bought the tickets until my parents phoned me the next day to say I'd won A MASSIVE BOX OF CHEESE!! I was so excited when they dropped it at my house for me. It had cheese, chutneys, crackers and all sorts of tasty goodies inside. They could've kept it and just eaten the cheese themselves but they didn't. Which was very Gouda them!"

So I had Davy, Andy Mills and Cooper & Davies along with the regular format of the event including an auction and raffle. As Davy was away on tour I was not able to host the event on World Cancer Day as before. We pushed the event back to allow him to join us as he really wanted to be there.

Selfie frames were very much in at the time of the third event and I managed to get one. Social media was really taking off at this time and everyone wanted to be part of it, sharing their thoughts and pictures and products, so I created a frame design and had it made. I wanted to have a nice little personal touch for Mum so I had the likes and reactions on it read as Mums date of birth. We still have it at events now. Many people have had their photo in it. We also had our logo emblazoned on the pub window created by a local artist, which was a really nice touch.

The wrist bands went down a storm at the last event so we had them at this one too. The bands proved to still be popular and were called them 'Bands against Cancer' for world cancer day and there was a #wecan or #ican, used by cancer charities at the time – as in 'we can or I can' beat cancer, which I incorporated into our third event when publicising it using the hashtag on our socials.

On the evening itself one of the guys who regularly drank in The Red Barn set up a lighting rig for us around the area where the bands were playing which gave a nice element to the stage area. I was very grateful for that. The night was really busy and people were up dancing again. Mandy, Davy's wife, created some new t-shirts for us, the bar staff, the band and I all wore them.

Family members and Carly, who was attending her first event, took care of the raffle tickets in Mums memory. I don't think Carly knew what she was letting herself in for. She was overwhelmed by the amount of people who attended. My sister Sally got a helium balloon with my Mums face on it which was a nice touch given we had lost her but could still have her in the room with us.

"Mark and I was officially a couple by the third event" added Carly. "Mark often joked how I was the official photographer as I am always tasked with setting up the social media and sorting out the prizes. As soon as we arrive at the venue we set up the prizes to make sure they are ready for people to see. Then and another joke, I am responsible for selling the raffle tickets. Strip after strip, from one person to the next and not stopping until the raffle takes place. There are always a few late comers who want tickets."

"The raffle is always really busy with so many prizes, and as Mark pulls the winning tickets I have to keep up with which prize goes with which ticket, and who had the ticket. It is a pet peeve of mine as Mark knows. And I always like to moan about the amount of raffle prizes we have, but then if we didn't we wouldn't raise so much money. I tease him though and tell him every year he needs to rethink how the raffle is run. I think he likes to tease me back and gets even more prizes! He even bought me a bum bag to keep the tickets and cash in!"

Davy also donated an acoustic guitar which he played on the evening and signed it for the auction. We also had bigger and better prizes than the year before; we had UK paintball supporting us along with Shrewsbury Town Football Club. It is one of the events where my memories are really strong not just because of the amount we raised, but because Mum wasn't there and I had Carly by my side and she hasn't left my side since. It was at this point things started to really grow as the prizes were better and the amount raised was more.

"CCC3 was a busy night and neither of us was expecting the amount of people that were there" said Carly. "It was such a good vibe with people laughing, dancing and spending money on the auction. I don't think I sat down all night. I took my family along to the event but I was so busy I didn't get to speak to them at all that night. The music was incredible; the auction raised a lot of money."

"After the raffle and auction, I tidied up and cleared away the prizes that were to be collected later, whilst Mark enjoyed his Guinness and chatted. I do get to enjoy a wine later at Mark's expense. My favourite role is counting the money the next morning. Despite playing various roles at the event I never take any credit as this is Marks event. I am quite happy to be in photos but always in the background as Mark should have the recognition for what he does."

"As CCC has grown my role hasn't changed that much. I guess as the events have become bigger he has gently handed over some of the reins to me so I can do more. As time has passed our understanding of each other has grown, as have our roles within the event. Everyone is doing their part and as each event gets closer the stress builds and I often get stressed over Marks laid back approach."

"He likes to pile the prizes on our dining table and our dining room becomes a bit of a CCC hub for a few weeks after Christmas. We both work full time but I don't think Mark realises that CCC becomes full time and trying to fit it all in can be difficult. Collecting prizes, printing off ones that have been emailed; sorting equipment we might need such as raffle tickets, merchandise etc. It's not only timely, but costly. Mark spends hours emailing, planning and promoting which can eat into family life which is something that not everyone sees, and especially with the events becoming so much more than they were in the early days they can become a real strain."

"One of my funniest memories is from CCC3." added Carly. "Davy who performed at the event was flying back to Dublin the next morning. After too many tequilas he had to be dragged from his bed and driven with minutes to spare to the railway station to get the train back to Birmingham airport. We are pleased to say he made the flight by the skin of his teeth, Davy did report it was his most difficult flight ever but I won't go into details as to why as he will never forgive me! I have some amazing photos of that evening with Davy and Mark singing and dancing in Marks living room, Davy trying to teach Mark how to catch the right beat on Mark's triangle, after all Mark is always boasting about his ability to play well."

Mark Fielden   137

"Andrea's hats bring fond memories too. She buys a new one every year to each event. They often end up being ripped off her head a passed around the pub for people to pose with for photos. I think she has lost a couple over the years too."

It was around this time that I found out that Toys R Us was closing. Unfortunately I lost the store where I had worked for over 21 years. So I lost my Mother, I lost my store and I lost my job, it was a very difficult time. However it was also a very proud time. We were able to put on the event and raised even more money than we had done previously, a staggering £1875! I remember counting the money and was not only super proud but completely blown away.

Carly and I went to Lingen Davies with a giant cheque for them. We met the team and have gotten to know them over the years. That was the start of a lovely relationship and friendship with the charity. After that event I was contacted by Lingen Davies to ask if were able to help with national volunteers week. In return we had our logo all over their website and social media presence saying what we had done and how much we had raised. That was a really good moment for me after such a heart-breaking year. That was definitely the toughest year of my life.

11

A Beautiful Way

The third event was a real turning point. After the success of the third event at The Red Barn, the new landlady of The Inn on the Green, Rachael, wanted the event to return home, so to speak. She was really helpful and when I explained what I wanted to do she said 'Yep no problem at all.' The event was booked in with her for the 9th February. Our overall grand total was £3380 and I wanted to exceed that with event four.

I launched the event on our FB page a little earlier to give me more time to get some good prizes for the auction. I also wanted to extend and grow the event. Andy Mills and Davy were willing to play again. We also had a new edition to the line up with a guy called Graham Clews. He was a very talented performer. I asked Cooper & Davies again and although they were still playing themselves as a duo they had also set up a band with other friends in Bridgnorth and called themselves The Beautiful Ways. The band was delighted to perform. This really enhanced our musical offering.

I decided that as we were ramping things up and the event was taking a more polished image that we needed a more professional looking poster. The previous posters were okay but were not really how I wanted them to be as I had done them myself. The new poster was designed by Jenny, a good friend of mine, and incorporated everything that we were about including all the acts.

It was also time to ramp up the advertising too now that the event was more established. More people needed to know who and what we were, why we were raising money and who for. This was the first year that we got a proper mention in the press, Shrewsbury Now newspaper, with a full page feature. I was really excited to see the feature when it dropped through the letterbox. My journey with the Shropshire Magazine started around this time too. I got in touch with the magazine about what we were doing and asked if they would like to feature us to which they said yes. We had a one page spread. It began to really feel like we were really getting somewhere now.

"When I see the room full of people listening to the music, I have to take a moment to think about what we've done, given people a good night and raised money for charity at the same time. It makes all the hard work and graft even more worthwhile."

Shropshire Magazine

Suddenly a big opportunity came along. I was using Twitter and Instagram a bit more so I got in touch with Radio Shropshire about what I was doing. They invited me along to the studio! I was super excited. The day of my visit arrived; I went to the studio not knowing what to expect. I was sat in the green room waiting for the producer to come and get me. It became a bit of a whirlwind at that point. Before I knew it I was sat in front of the presenter, headphones on with a mic in front of me. I remember thinking *'oh my goodness me what am I going to do here?'* but without further ado he introduced me live on Radio Shropshire across the airwaves!

It was a very proud moment and I was trying my best not to do any ums, err, ahhs, and apparently I did quite well. At one point I was using my hands to describe a prize, and suddenly realised that being on radio the listeners could not see what I was doing! I talked about CCC for at least 30 minutes live on air. I came out on a real high and received many nice messages from people about it. One comment did make me laugh saying I had a great face for radio, which I had to think twice about as nobody sees your face on the radio! It felt that momentum for the event was really building now, especially with the advertising for it and getting the name out there.

The Shrewsbury Biscuit Podcast also invited me to talk about the event. I spoke about my reasons for putting this amazing thing together and the important lessons that I have learnt in the 4 years of organising this.

I decided to approach a local venue in Shrewsbury called Albert's Shed. Albert's Shed in Shrewsbury and Telford's Southwater are the premier live music venues in Shropshire. Albert's mission is to champion grassroots music locally and beyond.

I spoke to David the owner, and he said that he would like to help my cause so over the course of the 25th and 26th January they held a Chords Crush Cancer weekend. They advertised it all across social media along with my story and what we were up to.

They had buckets on the doors and the Shed's customers raised £417 for us. I was delighted. I went back and had some photos taken and a beer, I was so pleased to have another local venue involved. So even before our event had even taken place I had media coverage, magazine coverage, been on the radio and had a fundraising weekend at a local bar.

We had new t-shirts designed for the event. The musical line up was Graham Clews, Andy Mills, Davy Lewis and The Beautiful Ways. Clive Pritchard of Clive's Caricatures joined us to provide artistic, entertaining and amusing cartoons of the guests. The auction had attracted great prizes. One prize was a replica Football World Cup 66 shirt, which was of course when England last won the World Cup and it was even signed by Sir Jeff Hurst. We had a log cabin along with hot tub overnight stay donated and the Birmingham Bears Cricket team donated two tickets to their game.

Mark Fielden 143

Dean Henderson, goalkeeper for Man United donated a signed pair of his Umbro gloves and Shrewsbury Town supported us yet again. We even had a bespoke guitar designed with an under the sea theme with a message in a bottle. It was beautiful and generated a lot of interest. We were given some tickets from the Professional Darts Corporation for the Premier League of Darts as well.

Comedian Carl Hutchinson donated tickets to his show at Theatre Severn in Shrewsbury. I had contacted him after seeing him as the support act for Chris Ramsey when Carly and I went to Chris' show. Carl was absolutely hilarious; we enjoyed him so much that we purchased tickets for his own show right there and then on the evening!

On the evening of 23/3/19 Carl invited us backstage into his dressing room before the gig where Carly and I, along with the two winners of the tickets from CCC4, chatted with him and his support act Anth Young. They were both very engaging, took an interest about CCC and posed for a few photos. I presented Carl with a CCC T-shirt which he changed into so he could match my top for a photo for my charity social media pages.

It was getting towards show time so we said our goodbyes and made our way to our seats, on the front row! Carl's support act Anth was absolutely brilliant, we had never seen him before but he got the crowd buzzing ready for Carl to take centre stage. Imagine my surprise and delight when Carl took to the stage wearing none other than my CCC T-shirt! I looked at Carly, tapping her arm and pointing at him with a huge grin on my face! This was incredible! Carl's performance was again brilliant; we, our CCC winners, and the rest of the audience had a right giggle!

Since then Carl has really taken off as a top notch comedian and his popularity has soared, but he's always been kind enough to reply to my messages and donated tickets to his other shows as prizes. Carl has recently started recording his own Podcast which is brilliant; I've often had a few strange looks come my way on the walk to work as I've been laughing along whilst listening. I've shared links to it via my charity social media pages to repay the support he gives to us, something small but a gesture all the same.

Mark Fielden   145

Anth is always generous with his words about our fundraising, and we enjoy a chat over Facebook now and then, more often than not about his own comedy shows and of course his beloved dog! When in Shrewsbury, Carl and Anth will always meet up for a chat after the gig and pose for a few photos, two fantastic comedians who have become good friends of Chords Crush Cancer, I'm very grateful to them both for their support.

"I first met Mark a few years ago now," said Hutchinson. "I was touched by his story and was very pleased to meet him at the show. His enthusiasm for the cause really shone through him and it's hard not to feel inspired when someone undertakes such a selfless act like Mark has."

"I was more than happy to wear the t-shirt on the night and take a few photos. I feel very privileged that my job allows me to make people happy and gives them a nice little memory to assist them through certain dark points of their life."

That night we raised a total of £2541.81 smashing the £5k target. It was at that point I thought *'Wow we have something really special here, how can we raise even more money for such a wonderful charity.'*

12

Bigger and Better

After such a successful fourth event, we had raised a total of £6776.85. I decided to launch the Facebook page on July 4th, which was much earlier than I had previously been doing as I really wanted to hit the £10k mark. I thought I would advertise the event as our 5th birthday. My friend Robbie from Ireland came up with an idea to have the hash tag #5for10 meaning the 5th event and hoping to take the total raised past £10k.

In terms of the line-up, we had Andy Mills, Davy Lewis and The Beautiful Ways band. We had T-shirts made again with the #5for10 logo on them. We also had some CCC beer mats made. Carly and I went to Majorca in the September for a long weekend so we took some with us. Whilst we handed them out in the Irish bar we got chatting to a few people and were able to spread the word about CCC which was great. This always used to make Carly laugh/cringe that I took the beer mats away with us, and also to various day trips – I still have some left and take them with me when we go away!

I also had some pens made this year with CCC#5for10 and sold them on Facebook and on the evening. I also handed some out during the promotional period. I was interviewed again on BBC Radio Shropshire which was fantastic publicity, and Alex from the Biscuit podcast also had me back on his show. Again, I had coverage in the local newspaper and Shropshire Magazine did a two-page spread on the event, which gave some really good publicity.

The quality of prizes this time around had really ratcheted up. Some highlights for me were Britain's Got Talent winner Kojo donated tickets to his show in Shrewsbury. Kojo Anim is a comedian who reached the final of series 13 of Britain's Got Talent. He originated from Ghana, however moved to London. We had Glee Comedy tickets from the Comedy Club and Go Below underground exploring. At Go Below in Snowdonia, you can test your nerve via a series of exciting adventurous challenges, including zip-lining through caverns, climbing up a vertical shaft, boating across a lake, traverse over an abyss, scale a waterfall or abseil your way down to the deepest point in the UK!

We also had I Fly Manchester donate an indoor skydiving experience; we had a bungee jump and tickets to the Shrewsbury Flower show. I went along to the flower show and met Chef John Torode who signed a copy of his book, it was fantastic to meet him. Jenny who made the guitar previously made a ukulele for us. Keeping with football we had a signed shirt that Carlton Morris of Shrewsbury Town had worn at Wembley. We had a helicopter tour and a Shrewsbury Prison tour as well. I must not forget the annual Shrewsbury football club signed shirt. The quality of the prizes this time was brilliant.

For me the prize that I was ecstatic about was the one from comedian Chris Ramsey as he was participating in Strictly Come Dancing at the time. I had messaged him on Twitter and he replied. I ran down the stairs with a huge grin on my face shouting Chris Ramsey has just messaged me. The kids were like "What? No way!!" I was on a massive high, running around the house. He has continued to support us since and he even bought me a pint of Guinness during the middle of one of his shows. That particular day I had just lost my job at Toys R Us and been looking after the kids all day, so I was tired and not in the best of moods. That evening we had planned to go to one of his shows at the Theatre Severn in Shrewsbury.

Having made a few jokes about me after picking me out of the audience, he came down off stage to give me a cuddle and said, "I'll buy you a pint at the end of the show." I shouted out "Guinness!" and he sent one of his team along with a pint during the middle of the show which was an absolute treat for me.

That moment really sticks in my mind. If I were to do a top 5 of memories with CCC that would be one of them. Chris Ramsey, smashing strictly and messaging "little old me" Mark from Shrewsbury – absolutely brilliant!

We also organised a quiz which I had never done before as a warm up event on February 6th with our main event being on the 8th February. It was at one of our local pubs, The Dolphin. We also sold raffle tickets and provided the prizes for 1st, 2nd and 3rd place winners. We raised a couple of hundred pounds that evening and raised awareness of the event to different people who may not have been aware of CCC. There we representatives of Lingen Davies there too. At the time I was working at Home Bargains, so there was a team from there as well. I felt really supported which contributed to me enjoying hosting the quiz and it's definitely something I would like to do again.

The 8th of Feb was upon us and the event was by far the busiest. We ended up raising £2790.43, which added to the money raised at the quiz, took us well past the £10k mark, I know the quality prizes for the raffle and the auction contributed. I must not forget local company Lefevre Chocolate, who got in touch after hearing our story and what we are about. Known for their artisan Belgian handmade truffles, they made a life-sized guitar cake with all the acts who sang on it. We were able to share it with everyone who came on the evening. To see the size of the guitar was amazing!

On 18th July 2019 I was invited to the Lingen Davies annual awards and presented with a Ruby Badge for all my fundraising. It was a lovely touch and it was lovely evening meeting other fundraisers who were raising money for the same charity.

Mark Fielden

13

The Pandemic

Sadly the 6th event had to be postponed as the country went into lockdown due to the Covid pandemic. But I had that itch; I still wanted to be fundraising somehow.

On 12 January 2020, the World Health Organization (WHO) confirmed that a novel coronavirus was the cause of a respiratory illness in a cluster of people in Wuhan City, Hubei, China, which was reported to the WHO on 31 December 2019. The fatality ratio for COVID-19 was significantly greater, with a significant total death toll. The COVID-19 pandemic in the United Kingdom was part of the worldwide pandemic of coronavirus disease 2019 (COVID-19) caused by severe acute respiratory syndrome coronavirus 2 (SARS-CoV-2). In the United Kingdom, it resulted in 24,680,566 confirmed cases, and is associated with 228,802 deaths.

The virus began circulating in the country in early 2020, arriving primarily from travel in Europe. The first wave was at the time one of the world's largest outbreaks. A legally-enforced stay at home order, or lockdown, was introduced on 23 March, banning all non-essential travel and contact with other people, and shut schools, businesses, venues and gathering places.

People were told to keep apart in public. Those with symptoms, and their households, were told to self-isolate, while those considered at highest risk were told to shield. The health services worked to raise hospital capacity and established temporary critical care hospitals, but initially faced some shortages of personal protective equipment. By mid-April it was reported that restrictions had "flattened the curve" of the epidemic and the UK had passed its peak after 26,000 deaths.

Restrictions were lifted in May and replaced with specific regional restrictions. Further nationwide restrictions were introduced later in 2020 in response to a surge in cases. The peak had passed and restrictions were gradually being eased but a second wave, with a new variant that originated in the UK became dominant and was deadlier than the first.

By the autumn, COVID-19 cases were again rising. This led to the introduction of social distancing measures and some localised restrictions. Larger lockdowns took place in all of Wales, England and Northern Ireland later that season. In both England and Scotland, tiered restrictions were introduced in October and England went into a month-long lockdown during November followed by new tiered restrictions in December.

Multi-week 'circuit-breaker' lockdowns were imposed in Wales and Northern Ireland. A new variant of the virus is thought to have originated in Kent around September 2020. Once restrictions were lifted, the novel variant rapidly spread across the UK. Its increased transmissibility contributed to a continued increase in daily infections that surpassed previous records. The healthcare system had come under severe strain by late December. Following a partial easing of restrictions for Christmas, all of the UK went into a third lockdown. The second wave peaked in mid-January with over 1,000 daily deaths, before declining into the summer.

The UK's overall death toll and by population surpassed that of Italy on 3 May, making the UK the worst affected country in Europe at the time. Restrictions were steadily eased across the UK in late spring and early summer that year. The UK's epidemic in early 2020 was at the time one of the largest worldwide.

The UK started a COVID-19 vaccination programme in early December 2020. Generalised restrictions were gradually lifted and were mostly ended by August 2021.

A third wave, fuelled by the new Delta variant, began in July 2021, but the rate of deaths and hospitalisations was lower than with the first two waves – this being attributed to the mass vaccination programme. By early December 2021, the Omicron variant had arrived, and caused record infection levels.

A third wave of daily infections began in July 2021 due to the arrival and rapid spread of the highly transmissible SARS-CoV-2 Delta variant. However, mass vaccination continued to keep deaths and hospitalisations at much lower levels than in previous waves. Infection rates remained high and hospitalisations and deaths rose into the autumn. In December, the SARS-CoV-2 Omicron variant was confirmed to have arrived and begun spreading widely in the community, particularly in London, driving a further increase in cases that surpassed previous records, although the true number of infections was thought to be higher. It became mandatory for people to show proof of full vaccination or proof that they are not infected to enter certain indoor hospitality and entertainment venues.

In response to the COVID-19 pandemic in the United Kingdom, the UK Government introduced various public health and economic measures to mitigate its impact. The government had developed a pandemic response plan in previous years. In response to the first confirmed COVID-19 cases in January 2020, the UK introduced advice for travellers coming from affected countries in late January and February 2020, and began contact tracing, although this was later abandoned. Parliament introduced the Coronavirus Act 2020, which granted the devolved governments emergency powers and empowered the police to enforce public health measures.

The UK government's response to the pandemic, in particular the timeliness of public health measures being introduced and lifted, has faced criticism from academic medical sources, media outlets, relatives of COVID-19 patients and various political figures. This criticism continued amid the Party gate scandal, as multiple government officials were revealed to have breached COVID-19 social distancing restrictions during lockdowns. A public inquiry into the response was established in June 2022.

The COVID-19 pandemic led to the largest fall in life expectancy in England since records began. On average, British COVID-19 victims lost around a decade of life; the last time deaths rose so sharply in the UK was during World War II. In 2020, the disease was the leading cause of death among men, and second leading cause among women.

The pandemic's major impact on the country's healthcare system, leading to long waiting lists for medical procedures and ambulances, also led to an indirect increase in deaths from other conditions. It also had a huge mental health impact.

The pandemic was widely disruptive to the economy of the United Kingdom, with most sectors and workforces adversely affected. Some temporary shutdowns became permanent; some people who were furloughed were later made redundant. The economic disruption has had a significant impact on people's mental health.

As I was unable to host another fundraising event, I came up with the whacky idea of putting an album or CD together. I came up with the idea during lockdown.

The COVID pandemic had a profound effect on the music industry, fundamentally changing the way music is created, performed, and experienced. Live music events and concerts were cancelled or postponed, leaving both musicians and audiences without a way to connect.

Music venues were closed, leaving many independent artists without their main source of income. The lack of physical interaction also had an effect on the creative process, with musicians needing to find innovative ways to collaborate and work remotely. This caused many artists to turn to digital streaming platforms and online performances, as well as creative approaches such as virtual concerts and live streams, in order to stay connected with their fans.

This resulted in an increase in digital listening experiences. The wide-reaching effects of the pandemic also caused a shift in music styles, with more artists embracing acoustic sounds that are easier to record from home. The pandemic caused a huge disruption in the music industry, but it also created opportunities for creative exploration and adaptation, with many musicians and other industry professionals focusing on creating more meaningful digital experiences for their fans, rather than simply relying on live performances.

I contacted my musician friends to ask if they would donate one of their original songs to the album. My friends agreed. I then put a message out to the wider community who I sort of knew, all of whom said yes. Could Chords Crush Cancer become Chords Crush Covid?!

I ended up with 17 tracks, including a British artist I had seen perform on holiday in Lanzarote, a guy I had seen playing in Ireland and a former Shrewsbury Town football player. It took a lot of hard work as it was something I had never thought about or done before.

I managed to pull the album together within 3 weeks! I had the idea to use the power of music to bring the country together as we were in lockdown and many had sadly lost loved ones. I decided to call the album 'Together' using the hash tag #songsforourfrontlineheroes to raise money for the NHS. When the CDs arrived it was amazing to see the idea actually in my hand. I immediately wanted to play it and wow it was brilliant. To hear these tracks from my friends and people I knew was remarkable. I'm still not sure now how I managed to do it.

I set up Facebook, Twitter and Instagram pages to promote our story and a website that enabled me to get the music onto platforms like Apple Play, iTunes and Spotify. I also added it to TikTok so you could choose a track on there to add to your TikTok creations/videos which proved to be very popular during lockdown especially.

I did my usual publicity drive and made it onto BBC Radio Shropshire, BBC News even featured it on their news page. I was also featured on signal 107 Wolverhampton. It was amazing what the power of music could do to raise money for our front line heroes who sacrificed so much during Covid. I also wanted to try to bring a bit of joy to those stuck at home during the pandemic getting fed up.

I was working at Home Bargains at the time and worked right through the pandemic. We launched the album on 2nd May. My friend Davy was doing a weekly live feed from his living room which he called 'Live from the Lounge' to keep people entertained so he launched the album using his song 'Hold On' which is the first track on the album which he played live.

People looked forward to his performances at the weekend. They would watch him with a beer in hand. It must have been a surreal experience for him being sat in his living room pelting out his songs being streamed on Facebook live. I was really grateful to Davy for doing that. He showed viewers what the CD looked like and where to download it.

On 5th May Andy Mills also held a live stream from his house and sang his song 'Mushroom House' that he donated to the album along with a lot of other songs for an hour long set. He set up a link for people to donate to our JustGiving page.

Rhi More the lead singer of The Beautiful Ways did a live set on 6th June again inviting people to donate and purchase a copy. When I look back at the time of the pandemic I think wow, not only was it very strange times that we were living in, but I worked full time, put together a CD and rose over £500 for the NHS. It was a shame we couldn't host the CCC event but it was just not safe to do so. I really enjoyed making the album and maybe one day I will create a CCC album from the artists who have performed for us over the years.

Chords Crush Cancer 5th Event

Guitar cake

Mark with Simon Davies

Caricaturist Clive

Mark on the mic

CC5 Cheque

STFC Shirts

Chords Crush Cancer 6th Event

Auction Items

CCC6 Beer mat promo

CCC6
Poster
Promo

Mark Fielden

CCC6 Promo

Carly, Anna LD
and Mark CCC6

Team CCC6

Andrea, Carly, Dave and Mark CCC Team 7

Memories of Margaret

Dad and Shropshire Magazine

Community Ambassador

Luke
Crump
guitar

Mark Fielden

Mark Shropshire Magazine

Wayne Rooney Shirt

Mark Fielden   175

Carly and Mark CC7 Cheque

Disney Banksy

Banksy

Me and Mum

Mum and Dad

Mark with John Torrode

Comedian Carl Hutchinson

Mark Fielden 183

14

Failure Does Lead to Success

The sixth event coincided with our second quiz night which we held a couple of nights before on the 3rd February 2022 at The Dolphin pub. The Dolphin was very accommodating. We provided prizes for the first, second and third place which is their bi weekly quiz. We also had raffle prizes and Carly went around with her trusted bum bag and card machines selling the tickets. We raised £175 on the evening. It was good to see some people form Lingen Davies and some of my old work colleagues from Home Bargains Shrewsbury there too and they actually won.

The sixth event was held on the 5th February 2022. We had the usual line up of raffle and auction, live music, Clive the caricaturist was back and we welcomed a new edition to the line up as Magic Martin a local close up magician joined us. I thought that would change things up a little bit. He was really well received. Some of his tricks were mind blowing.

The music line up was Rhi Moore the female vocalist from The Beautiful Ways, who has played for us before and Andy Mills. Davy Lewis sadly got covid and it was touch and go whether he would be able to perform. We held out to the last couple of days but he was still unwell so Rhi extended her set and Andy did a double set either side of the raffle and auction.

We were featured in My Shrewsbury Magazine for the first time. Shrewsbury Chronicle featured us again as did the Shropshire Star and Lingen Davies got involved this year. I went along to their offices to give the official launch and build up to the event. We took some photographs with Hannah of Lingen Davies with official posters of the event.

We had the beer mats with our branding on them sponsored by C2 Recruitment; we had t-shirts once again using the t-shirt design that Jenny had done for us and we featured on the Shrewsbury Biscuit Podcast again to give us a bit more promotion and to talk about how good it was to be back after the enforced break following covid. The Shropshire Star did an in depth article on us celebrating that we had raised over £14,000 in total. The event itself along with the quiz night raised £3,366.54 which took us to the £14,000 mark.

We had some big names supporting us. We had Clive Tildesey the football commentator, Phil 'The Power' Taylor a famous world champion darts player provided us with a signed framed t-shirt.

Mark Fielden   185

Terry Kneeshaw, an artist from Newcastle, donated David Bowie and Amy Winehouse prints which were both framed and signed by him. One of the big ones for me, in value anyway was a company called Ooni gave us a pizza oven which went down well in the auction. Comedians were supporting us in force again; Paul Merton gave tickets to his show, Joel Dommett donated tickets to his show, and we had some music and festivals supporting us. Camp Bestival gave us weekend passes, we had tickets to the 'In it Together' Festival and Lets Rock Shrewsbury Festival. Pop band The Enemy gave us tickets to their show, I remember growing up listening to them! We had a Harry Potter Studio tour in London donated by Experience Days; we also had sports memorabilia including a men's and women's team Trent Rockets signed cricket bat from The Hundred, along with a signed shirt. We had not had cricket items before so that was something different. Probably one of the best items we had ever had, local artist Luke Crump donated a bespoke guitar that he had designed specifically for Chords Crush Cancer. It had his trademark doodle drawings on it.

"I decided to support Chords Crush Cancer because it held a deeply personal significance for me" added Luke. "My grandma, or Nana Chester as she's known to us, has battled and overcome breast cancer in the past. Witnessing her strength and resilience during that difficult time left a lasting impact on me. I wanted to contribute to a cause that cares for, comforts and helps those also fighting this relentless disease."

"For my contribution to the fundraiser, I donated an original piece of my artwork: a fully customised electric 'doodle' guitar, featuring symbols of energy, music, love & positivity. My wish was to raise as much as possible for Lingen Davies and to also symbolise the power of music and art in healing. Being able to use my artistic voice to fight against cancer and help others who may be going through what my Nana Chester experienced was truly special!"

The night itself was rammed, really busy. The auction went really well and lots of people bought raffle tickets and had their caricatures done. Magic Martin went down an absolute storm. The night took us over the £14000 mark which was amazing. We came out of that on a massive high. It was great to be back!

I launched the seventh event on 4th May 2022 on Facebook with the event being held on World Cancer Day 4th Feb 2023. My target was to get as close as possible to £20k. It was a big ask. It was something I wanted to try to get to. However, over the years we have gained tremendous support from a whole host of famous names and companies – Chris Ramsey, Carl Hutchinson, Joel Dommett, Russell Kane, Bryan Adams, Sir Tom Jones, The Enemy, Bastille, Shed Seven, artist Terry Kneeshaw, Eve Jones, Phil Taylor, Gazza, Manchester United, Ooni Pizza Ovens, Cazoo and Camp Bestival to name just a few.

The build up to the event was really exciting. I featured on the front cover of Shropshire magazine which has a wide range of readers around Shrewsbury and Shropshire. It was quite funny how it came about; I emailed them as I had previously featured in the magazine promoting previous events. The features writer asked if I would I be able to meet her for an interview. I had changed job in November so was working at Primark. It was after Christmas and I was working nights. The morning of the interview I finished worked at 7am, but managed a couple of hours sleep before heading to The Inn on the Green for the interview.

She was really interested in what we were doing and I was sat with her for a good hour. Then a photographer turned up and he took various photos. Everyone in the pub was looking to see what was going on. I felt a bit like a celebrity!

A few weeks had passed and it was late January. I had popped to the local shop and whilst in the queue for the shopping I needed, I spotted a big dispenser with Shropshire Magazine emblazoned all over it. It had the Shropshire Star, our local newspaper on the top shelf then the bottom three shelves had my face looking back at me on the Shropshire Magazine. It was brilliant. I was like "WOW." I was full of emotion and pride to see myself on the front cover. It was unbelievable!

Heather Large, Senior features writer at Express & Star, Shropshire Star and Shropshire Magazine said "As soon as I spoke to Mark, I knew his story was one that would touch the hearts of our readers. Mark's achievements, his lovely words about his mother and the wonderful charity he is supporting is something my editor and I discussed at length and we were both in agreement that it was something to promote and support as much as possible."

"The in-depth interview with Mark covered all of the above ... but a picture tells a thousand words. Our photographer Jamie Ricketts captured Mark brilliantly and we quickly realised that the logo on Mark's shirt would clearly stand out on magazine stands across the county - so we knew that was the shot for the front cover."

Obviously I bought a copy of the magazine. When I got to the till I said to the cashier "It's not very often you see the same guy twice is it?" He looked a bit confused at first, and then looking at the front cover asked, "Is that you?" I said "Yeah" and had a little conversation with him about why I was on it.

Before I left I took a photo using the Snapchat App and sent it to Carly. As soon as I got home, I got her to take a picture of me with the magazine; I sent it to Dad and Sally even though I hadn't actually read the article. However it was a smashing article about what we were doing and why we were doing it and what we were hoping to achieve.

I wanted to do something different with the prizes for this event so I had the idea of having a signed football shirt from as many football clubs as possible. I contacted every club from the Premier League all the way down to the National League. Although I was excited, it didn't really pay off I did get one from Bournemouth, West Bromwich Albion and Stoke City along with the usual one from Shrewsbury Town. Well over half the teams never replied, a couple said that they would see what they could do but never came back to me. A bit of a failure to my grand plan but you have to try different ideas.

Having failed somewhat at the football t-shirt idea, I decided to go big on the comedy front and got a fantastic response. Simon Brodkin gave us tickets to his tour, Axle Blake who was the Britain's Got Talent winner 2022 sent us tickets to his tour. Gary Meakle, Chris McCowsland, Finn Taylor, Carl Hutchinson and Babatunde Aleshe of I'm A Celebrity...Get Me Out Of Here and Russell Kane also donated so some real big names.

We also had some great music prizes too, Bastille gave us tickets to their show at Ludlow Castle; a couple of bands who I was into when I was in 6th form college Shed Seven and Suede also gave tickets to their gigs. I was humbled to have such huge artists supporting us.

We had tickets to Karen's Diner for an experience dinner. You go to the diner and get treated like trash which is part of the evening and there was a lot of interest in that one. We had tickets from Go Below again and tickets for Ninja Warrior UK obstacle course. We had tickets from Urban Playground which is the home of ITV's Cube so you go and challenge yourself against the Cube. DJ Fat Tony signed his new book, which was really popular when I was trying to get hold of a copy. As did Dr Alex who is the UK mental health youth ambassador and former Love Island star.

We had tickets to the Heal festival, in Shrewsbury, where The Enemy where headlining. We had alpaca trekking and tickets to see Spitting Image live. We had a crimpet machine to make toasted sandwiches, and the main prize was a Wayne Rooney signed Manchester United shirt and Clive Tyldesley's commentary notes from the 2008 Champions League Final. The notes were also signed by commentator Clive Tyledesley.

Comedian MC Hammersmith also gave us tickets to his show. He does improvisation comedy by making up raps from items held up from the audience. He also did a rap about the event and posted it on his social media accounts which gave us some great exposure, as he is huge on both on TikTok and Instagram. "I decided to support Chords Crush Cancer because cancer has affected numerous people in my life" said Hammersmith. "My friendship groups and close family are littered with cancer patients and survivors. The sooner we get to eradicate this tragic illness the better."

In the April before the event I was invited to the annual Lingen Davies awards evening as we had been shortlisted in two categories – social engagement and community – we didn't win either but I was delighted to receive a commendation from them.

The event evening itself was really busy. It was absolutely chock-a-block in the pub. We had the usual live music. We had Andy Mills up first, followed by Cooper & Davies, then The Beautiful Ways. I had invited back Magic Martin and Clive the caricaturist, both of who were very busy on the night.

The Shrewsbury Biscuit Podcast interviewed me and some of the musicians and representatives from Lingen Davies at the event and released the podcast the day after.

It was really nice to sit with a glass of Guinness the next day and listen to some of the comments from guests. Alex launched a vlog for me with videos of the evening. It was brilliant what he had put together. Seeing and hearing what people had to say at the event was rather mind blowing.

When I see the room full of people listening to the music, watching the magic and having a caricature drawn, I have to take a moment to think about what we've done. People had a good night and raised money for charity at the same time. It makes all the hard work and graft even more worthwhile. We raised £4278.98 which was huge and took our grand total to over £19k.

"Mark as always been driven by his passion for the event and during 2022 we were planning our wedding too" added Carly. "We got married in April 2023 but not before CCC7 in the February. I did get a bit stressed with Mark telling him how I wished he put as much effort into the wedding planning as he did CCC 7, then the wedding prep would have been done months ago!"

"He promised that once the event was over he would give the wedding more attention, which he did, but CCC7 came first. I also told him that there was not be an event in 2023 because of the wedding but it went ahead anyway. I supported him of course but perhaps was a bit more stressed and aggravated than normal!"

Chords Crush Cancer was recognised for its fundraising at the annual Lingen Davies awards evening in 2020 when it was awarded the prestigious Errol Williams award. It has also been highly commended for two further awards. Head of fundraising Helen Knight says "It is thanks to the hard work and dedication of supporters like Mark that the charity is able to continue supporting and enhancing local cancer services."

"As a charity we rely on the local community to support our vital cancer awareness raising work, and ensuring we can support the best possible cancer services at The Royal Shrewsbury Hospital and rehabilitation in the wider community. People throughout Shropshire and Mid Wales will benefit from our work and the efforts of Mark and the brilliant Chords Crush Cancer event. To have already raised more than £19,000 in memory of his mum Margaret is phenomenal."

15

Community Ambassador

A Lingen Davies celebration evening took place on 4th July 2023 at the Oswald street showground. I received a 'Save the Date' postcard about it. A few days later I received a letter from Helen Knight, Head of fundraising at Lingen Davies informing me that I had been nominated for an award for all the hard work that I have done with Chords Crush Cancer, promoting Lingen Davies and raising money. I was absolutely delighted.

I changed my shifts at work and made sure Carly was free so we could both go along. The evening of the event, we were greeted at the showground by some of the volunteers of Lingen Davies who gave us a beer as we arrived. We took our seats in a lovely room with lots of round tables. On the table was the order of the evening including what awards were up for grabs. I was sat next to Alex Whitely from the Shrewsbury Biscuit Podcast who has interviewed me a few times. He was there with his wife, we all quickly started chatting. There were 170 volunteers, fundraisers and supporters who had all been invited to the celebration.

"We believe in recognising the hard work and dedication of everyone involved with the charity" added Anna Williams. "Whether someone donates £1, £1,000 or £10,000, or an hour or more of their time, every single person in our community has a role to play in helping us support cancer services - we ALL know someone who will be impacted by cancer in their lifetimes. We want to celebrate this achievement by the wider Lingen Davies community."

"Eryl Williams was the long-serving Appeal Manager of the charity helping to generate millions of pounds for local patients. Eryl sadly passed away in 2012 after her own cancer diagnosis and four year treatment journey. The award was created to recognise Eryl's passion, determination and long lasting legacy to Lingen Davies, and is given annually to those supporters who mirror those qualities."

"Mark's enthusiasm, endless drive to source amazing prizes for Chords Crush Cancer, and commitment to the charity exemplify everything about the Eryl Williams award. By the end of next February he will have helped raise more than £20,000 for us – a phenomenal achievement and incredible legacy to pass on."

Mark Fielden   197

"We are strong believers in supporting our supporters. We attend as many events as we can, talk to our third-party fundraisers; help assist people with bucket collections, birthday collections, online donations, and generally do whatever people need us to do to make their events a success. We offer wider marketing and promotion of people's challenges, achievements, and endeavours through our social media channels, and we ALWAYS say thank you to each and every one of our wonderful fundraisers."

"I was fortunate enough to attend this year's Chords Crush Cancer in February. A group of us went from work in our own time and had a brilliant night supporting Mark, helping to boost the figure from auction prizes, dancing, joining in with the magic tricks, and chatting to Mark's family and friends who attended. More of us will be going next year – it's a great fundraiser and definitely puts the fun in fund raising."

Prior to the award ceremony, Lingen Davies gave an overview of what had been happening with the charity over the year, and then the awards began. It was inspiring to hear about others and what they had been doing and why they were helping the charity. Each section was broken down and the nominees had their photo projected onto a screen. The Master of Ceremonies read out some nice words about who they were, what they had done and why they were supporting Lingen Davies.

The winner was then announced and invited up onto the stage to collect a nice certificate. The nominees were also invited up which I thought was a very nice touch. Before we got to our category, we had a lovely meal which included cake for dessert. The bar was open for beers and people were talking. The room was abuzz with conversation, I introduced myself to people I didn't know, it was a really lovely evening.

We got to the category that I was nominated for which was the Community Ambassador Award. I was up against Alex Whitley, AICO ltd and Colin Boar who is out in the community sharing Lingen Davies posts on social media. It was a very tough category as our stories were shared; I was really delighted to be nominated. The winner was then announced, and I was amazed when I heard my name read out. I wore a beaming smile as I made my way to the stage to collect my award.

"Mark won the Community Ambassador Award this year" added Williams. "This is a new category introduced for 2023 to recognise the work Mark – and a few others in our community – do to highlight and promote the work of Lingen Davies in their own time."

Mark Fielden   199

"It's not just about fundraising; it's about promoting us to wider audiences – whether that's in person, online, through social media, in the local media, or through projects such as this book. Mark is a true Lingen Davies ambassador through and through and we are honoured to have him alongside us."

Afterwards I had some professional photos taken of me with my award and then with the other nominees. It was inspiring to be in a room with such amazing people, all of whom do varied and different fundraising and work for Lingen Davies, and to hear their story of why they do it.

There were many in the room that have cancer or have been treated by Lingen Davies and are still alive because of the fundraising I and others do to raise funds to help these people. I felt very proud to be amongst such wonderful people. Obviously I was delighted to win the award and what an award it is: The Community Ambassador of the Year for Lingen Davies. Wow!!

When I got home I showed the kids the certificate and sent a picture to my Dad and sister. I sat down with a beer to reflect upon what that meant and what we had achieved to be recognised by the charity. I posted about it on social media and had some really lovely comments such as 'you really deserve it.' Mum would be very proud of all the work that I have put in and to have won an award of such a strongly worded title – Community Ambassador Award. It is something that I am very, very proud of.

16

Onward

As part of the Shrewsbury Art Trail some guerrilla art appeared on the wall of the market hall. Now in its third year, the Shrewsbury Arts Trail continues to grow. With a passion for art and the desire to make art accessible to a larger community while at the same time promoting the work of local artists, the small but dedicated Arts Trail team is led by founder, Jess Richards.

An original piece of art was created by anonymous artist Disney. He has been dubbed as the 'Birmingham Banksy' as his style is very similar to Banksy and his artwork has popped up all over the Midlands.

His first piece of art appeared in Shrewsbury during October 2022 on the old British Telecom building. It caught my eye and I began following him on Instagram. Another piece popped up on 3rd July 2023 but was removed within 24hours so not many people got to see it.

There was a post about it being removed on Instagram, so I replied in the comments that I would really love a piece of his artwork to be donated to us, for our auction. I explained who we were, what we were doing and how much we have risen. He replied saying that he had previously helped raise £600 for the Princess Trust. That was to make wigs of real hair for girls with cancer. He messaged me directly to say that he had a piece ready for me and that he would be in Shrewsbury soon but never gave a date or time, it was all rather mysterious.

One day a piece of art suddenly appeared on the market hall wall in Shrewsbury, and I soon got another message saying the artwork was ready for me to collect at a secret location. I was at work at the time so I took my lunch break and went to the location that had been agreed. I was quite nervous, was I actually going to come face to face with the Birmingham Banksy, or not?

When I arrived, I was excited and nervous at the same time, but managed to get hold of the artwork. I didn't get to meet the Birmingham Banksy, Disney himself though. The artwork was amazing; I wasn't expecting it to be so big to be honest. It was the same size as what was spray painted onto the wall so an exact replica on an acrylic board. I took it back to work and people were like 'What is that?'

Mark Fielden   203

I explained and then showed them an article that had been in the local paper the Shropshire Star. I contacted Meghan at the Shropshire Star and asked her if she would like to do a follow up story on this. She came back to me with 'Yes we'd love to'. So between her and the management of the market hall we arranged a photo shoot. I went to the market hall with Carly and the print, and we had some professional photos taken for the newspaper.

We stood the acrylic board next to the artwork on the wall for a couple of photos, and then went inside for a coffee. I met Sarah, the social media manager for the market hall, who also did an interview with me about the event, and how I got the artwork. She wrote a lovely piece on Facebook about it. It's created a lot of interest so I have high hopes for it and hope it will beat the amount raised via the Wayne Rooney shirt.

It has created a lot of interest around Shrewsbury. The Shrewsbury Art trail shared it on Instagram stories, as did the artist Disney himself and he has a lot of followers. People are really interested in his work and to get hold of an original piece is really good for us.

Carly and I were talking about prizes and what we had got so far. I was throwing around different ideas of what I was looking for next and suddenly Carly laughed at me. She said "Mark, what you've got is amazing, a limited-edition Banksy style piece of art Wow!" Now Carly doesn't always get as excited about prizes as I do but you could tell that she thinks that this is one hell of a prize. The more I think about it the more I agree with her. Me just being me and messaging the artist who could quite of easily have said no but luckily for me he didn't.

So here we are with an amazing, limited edition, very rare piece of artwork that could potentially make a lot of money for the charity. It's certainly one I am keeping my eye on. I put it on our page on Instagram and since then I have seen our followers increase; our traffic has increased as has the overall reach of our social media. I am really excited about that one, it's so unique.

Over the years I have learnt that quality over quantity is the way forward. Looking back at the early events, the prizes I got were more about quantity. The prizes were not great, Xbox games, boxes of chocolates, bottles of wine, that type of thing but now we get some real high profile prizes from those who are classed as celebrities, from sports, television, media and comedy.

Mark Fielden   205

I have definitely become better at this. We have 12 comedians giving to our next event, CCC8 in February 2024, including Michael Macintyre, Romesh Ranganathan, Troy Hawke, Ross Noble, Seann Walsh, Pete Firman, Gary Meikle, Carl Hutchinson, Phil Chapman and Viggo Venn. Acclaimed cartoonist David Squires has donated a signed print that he's shipping to us from Australia, we have tickets to some of the biggest music artists in the country courtesy of Cuffe and Taylor, and a fine dining experience in a restaurant that featured on BBC's MasterChef. We have diversified into different areas over the years to get better prizes. We now work with hotels and glamping; fine dining and log cabins with hot tubs are very popular. I would absolutely love to get a holiday; I have contacted major airlines and holiday operators but had no success yet. I also contact people directly via email and on every social media channel. I break the prizes down into what I am looking to get, identify sectors and who to contact, starting in and around Shrewsbury and working out to the wider areas. I have found the area of Chester very accommodating as is Liverpool; I find it very tricky to get prizes in London.

The event has grown so much over the years, the prizes have become much better; the music has always been top notch and we have even added different acts to mix things up a little. We have added a caricaturist and magician, which have brought a totally different spectrum to the event. I have toyed with the idea getting a comedian as I have gotten to know a few over the years, but it depends if they are available and how much they charge as I want to make money, not spend it. To have a comedian open up the evening would certainly bring a new angle to the event.

Every event is a huge success for me but in terms of the biggest success, I think that would have to be the auction of the signed Wayne Rooney shirt, including the commentary notes from the Champions League final, which sold for over £300. I remember saying 'You are changing people's lives for the better' into the microphone as the bids kept rising. At our next event in 2024 we will have the amazing artwork from Disney, the 'Birmingham Banksy', and I can't wait to see how much that raises.

The current cost of living crisis has certainly had an impact on the events. Charities are being faced with increased demand as people look to organisations for support and advice and there has been a particularly steep increase in people seeking advice around money management, as well as the other challenges that can arise due to financial instability, such as mental health related issues.

The charity sector emerged from the pandemic during the first quarter of 2022 in better shape than expected, thanks to government grants and public and donor support. However, fast-forward to the second half of the year and returning optimism has dwindled as political instability, the cost-of-living crisis and soaring energy prices hit the UK, and once again charities find themselves under pressure to assist growing numbers of people.

As an indicator of the deteriorating situation, between August and October 2022, Citizens Advice referred 85% more people for emergency charity support or to food banks than in the same period in 2021, and 133% higher than two years ago. Whilst the number of people donating to charity fell by nearly four million in November, typically the peak month for giving.

When we came out of the pandemic many businesses were quick to offer prizes, whether that was to kick start the economy or to raise interest in their brands again. However, that has slowed right down now and businesses are being more stringent with who they are supporting. I find that I have to be very specific about what I am asking for, for them to say yes, however I still get many no's and even no reply at all, I have to be really thick skinned.

In terms of people supporting, they are still being very generous. However, I think people certainly think more about which events they chose to go to now. We are very lucky to have a loyal fan base that has built up over the years and who come out and support us. Even though the prizes are great, they are only worth what people are willing or can afford to bid so it's definitely had an effect.

I am so lucky to have the ongoing support from local businesses and talent. Caricaturist Clive Pritchard said "I have supported Mark's cause for the past few years and always look forward to returning. The charity is important to many as we all have been or know someone affected by cancer. The organisation that it takes to put on an evening of entertainment is immense."

"Mark and his team always deliver and it's always great to see the people who attend having a great night out while supporting the charity. It's been a pleasure to be a part of and I would like to congratulate Mark and his team for the last seven years and raising a phenomenal amount for his charity."

Magician Magic Martin said "Why did I choose Chords Crush Cancer? Firstly, this charity has been doing an incredible job of raising money for an important cause. Cancer has affected so many lives, including those of my loved ones. By supporting this charity, I feel like I am making a difference and contributing towards supporting those living with this devastating illness. It's inspiring!"

"Not only does performing my close-up magic for Chords Crush Cancer allow me to give back, but it also brings me a sense of joy and fulfilment. Seeing the smiles on people's faces as they watch my tricks is priceless. It's a wonderful feeling to know that I can brighten someone's day and hopefully this can ease a few more pounds into the kitty. Knowing that I am utilizing my skills to do something positive warms my heart, and it's an amazing way to spread some positivity and hope."

"My relationship with CCC is a win/win as I'm helping to raise funds, having an amazing time entertaining and making new friends all at the same time! It's quite a journey!"

"Each event brings so much variety and fun" adds Carly. "Not just from the night itself but also from the build-up. One memory that sticks in my mind is how we involve our children. As they have grown with the event over the years, they have wanted to become more involved and have taken a great interest which is so amazing to see. They have been to the Build a Bear shop and chosen a bear for name the bear. They also like to come up with ideas for the name of the bear and often come up with funny options."

"They have attended more events over the recent years as they have become older. They have bought raffle tickets with their pocket money and take a keen interest in some of the prizes. I love that Chords Crush Cancer inspires them as they tell their teachers and friends at school about it. Many of the teachers have heard of the event which shows just how big a part of the local community the event has become."

"There are lots of little memories too that stay with me, such as the balloon with Margaret's face on it flying high at the third event, people singing and dancing to the music. Mark's face when talking about his latest prizes, or fundraising ideas. I also enjoy listening to people who attended the events talk about them and how fantastic they were, the prizes and simply declaring they will be back for the

Mark Fielden

next one. The event gives me such an amazing feeling of pride, knowing that I have played a part in something that has made such a big difference to such a needed charity and to people's lives."

A recent survey by the Charities Aid Foundation (CAF) revealed that more than 50% of the UK's charities are digging into reserves; half fear they won't survive the cost-of-living crisis, and only 49% think they have enough funds to meet current demand.

Charities need to mitigate against a funding shortfall so it is expected that one key trend in 2023 will be income diversity, the need for charities to find various ways to raise funds, not simply relying on tried and tested (and often diminishing) channels. Charities need to increase the number of income streams.

Fundraising is hugely exciting, rewarding, and skilled, but it's also demanding, involving, and high pressured. For fundraisers to be able to do their best work for the causes and charities they choose to help, they need to make sure they are looking after their own wellbeing.

Fundraisers deal with a whole number of issues – the run up to a launch of a public appeal that has been months in preparation; the exposure and closeness to causes and beneficiaries and the emotions, some difficult conversations with supporters or others; as well as what's happening in their personal lives.

Just as we all have our own reaction to stress, we also have our own coping strategies; conscious or otherwise. They might include going out for a run or bike ride, playing music, going out with friends, spending time with family, watching a favourite TV show, reading a good book or in my case enjoying a cold pint of Guinness.

In terms of the Chords Crush Cancer brand, I am very proud of what we have built over the years. I think if you were to ask anyone in Shrewsbury if they had heard of it, I think most people would say yes. I really don't want to become stagnant, so after many years of doing an event in a pub with music, an auction, and a raffle, I think that now is the time for a change. As we are approaching the £20k mark, a huge milestone for us, I think CCC8 will be a fitting end to this format of fundraising.

Mark Fielden

The current format has nearly outgrown the venue, even though I am so grateful to be given the pub to host the event, the amount of people we have coming along means the pub is close to capacity with, at times, standing room only!

I have various ideas that keep entering my mind about how we can evolve and keep the fundraising going. How incredible would it be to host a large-scale festival, alongside other supporters of Lingen Davies Cancer Fund? That's a dream and a million miles away from what I do now, but I keep thinking to myself, *'would it be possible?'*

I've also toyed with the idea of hosting a comedy night, 'Chords Crush Cancer Comedy' or CCCC, and that's a lot of C's! I love watching live comedy myself, was a huge fan of Jethro before he sadly passed away, and via my fundraising events have made contacts with one or two of the UK's best comedians. I've already got a logo sorted for this, so it's something that I'm definitely considering.

Chords Crush Cancer 8
The Last Chapter

Inn On The Green
3rd February 2024 7pm

Auction & Raffle
Live Music
Clive's Caricatures
Magic Martin

Lingen
Davies

In Aid Of Lingen Davies
Cancer Fund 1160922

Andy Mills   The Shireish Rovers   Hot Rubber

Another idea would be to do some challenges; Lingen Davies has recently opened an office in Wales so I have thought about walking from the Shrewsbury office to the one in Wales, but I will have to do a bit of training for that, it would take around 13 hours looking at the map. Carly did laugh when I told her, but it would certainly grab people's attention!

Other challenges I have thought of include climbing Snowdon; Carly likes walking and often walks up hills so we could get the kids, family, friends and other supporters to join us.

What about shaving my beard off? Nah, that's just a stupid idea!

There are plenty of ideas we can look at.

Given the amount of effort it has taken to build the Chords Crush Cancer brand it would be a shame to stop, and after all it was created in Mum's memory.

So what is next? I'm not sure. What I can say is that Chords Crush Cancer has been an incredible journey, and one that I simply don't want to end.

I hope I have done you proud Mum, you are forever my inspiration and always in my heart.

Lingen Davies Cancer Fund exists to enhance cancer services and improve lives in Shropshire, Telford & Wrekin, and Mid Wales. Founded in 1979, with the aim of bringing cancer services to Shropshire for the first time, their work is now focused in three key areas: cancer prevention and early diagnosis, excellent treatment delivered locally, and living well with and beyond cancer.

I'd like to thank the whole team at Lingen Davies Cancer Fund for all their support with my Chords Crush Cancer events in memory of Mum.

"Enhancing cancer services and improving lives in our community."

The Fundraising Office,
Hamar Centre, Royal Shrewsbury Hospital, Mytton Oak Road, Shrewsbury, Shropshire, SY3 8XQ.
Tel: 01743 492396
Email: hello@lingendavies.co.uk
Registered Charity Number 1160922.

Sign post

Lingen Davies   www.lingendavies.co.uk

Breast Cancer Now www.breastcancernow.org

Macmillan   www.macmillan.org.uk

Marie Curie   www.mariecurie.org.uk

Cancer Research   www.cancerresearchuk.org

Mark Fielden

Printed in Great Britain
by Amazon

37047682R00126